The Gentle World of Childhood

Starting School in England

William Stephens

Sentry Press
Tallahassee, Florida
2001

Gentle World of Childhood: Starting School in England

Copyright © 1997, William N. Stephens

ISBN 1-889574-10-4
Library of Congress Number 2001 131009

www.wstephens.net

Back Cover: *Edna Ward on the day of her retirement.*

INTRODUCTION

Mossford Green Primary School still exists. There is a high wire fence around it now, and locks are on the gates. Edna and her teachers, and her children and their parents, have departed. The children grew up and sent her proud letters with photos of their own children. The older teachers retired. The parents gave us a warm welcome when we went back to visit. But now Edna herself has died.

Schools in England are different from what they were in Edna's time. When we interviewed across the country, we were told that she wouldn't have been able to do this today. There is too much bureaucracy.

The watershed year was 1989, when the National Curriculum was installed. Now there are countless reports and records to fill out, and prescribed items in the curriculum, to keep teachers and school Heads busy. Much time and anxiety goes into preparing for school inspections.

This is a tragedy, because remnants of the great educational tradition still exist. Here and there, teachers want to do some of these things. And they may even try to do them, working nights and weekends in order to fit everything in. When we inquired about the school in the village that Edna had moved to, we were told that it came close to the old ideal. This was because the teachers and Head were trying to do everything—satisfy the bureaucracy and teach to the children's needs.

TABLE OF CONTENTS

Chapter 1

STARTING SCHOOL

When would children start coming to school?

—As babies. Especially if they had a younger brother or sister who was already in school. Since babyhood, they had been coming with their mums to fetch their brothers or sisters home after school. And they would come with their mums to school assemblies and sports days and concerts. And they might come with an older brother or sister, and sit in the classroom with them for a short time.

Thursday was the day when mothers could bring their pre-schoolers to school assembly. So they became familiar with assembly and how school children behaved.

But every child, even if he had no older brother or sister, had to start visiting a year before he entered. He would start coming in for an afternoon, and that would build up to two afternoons per week, or an entire day. These children were just coming in for familiarization. There were no lessons for them. They were learning about where to go to the loo, and washing their hands. They were learning their way around the building. They were given a peg in the cloakroom to hang their coat on, and a locker to put their shoes in.

We were trying to give them a feel for the place, and a feeling of confidence, finding their way around.

(I remember when I myself started school, back home in America, long ago. That big building, those crowds, those bigger children—I thought, I'll never be able to find my way around. I felt so intimidated. I marveled at a little girl who seemed to know where to go.)

. . . So a new child pretty much knew what went on at school before he started; and he could find his way around. There was considerable anticipation too. I remember a parent saying once, about his little boy: "He's already saving for the school trip."

This preschool visiting was good for the teaching staff also. It worked both ways. They, too, became somewhat familiar with the new children. They knew the children's names, they met their mothers. They had formed some beginning impressions of the new children's personalities. They might have noted which children seemed particularly shy or, otherwise, which children might need special attention.

<u>Signing the register</u>

In the term before the child was to start school, his parents brought him to me, to have his name officially entered into the school register. Especially for children who had older brothers and sisters in school: they knew this was an important time.

They would be given a school pencil. I would tell him: "This is how you hold your pencil. . . . This is how you make your letters . . . ." and I wrote his name at the top of a pad of paper. This was to be his first school workbook. I wrote his name clearly, while he watched. Then I gave the pencil and workbook to him. He could practice writing his name at home. Hopefully, he would follow this example and hold his pencil properly.

And I would speak to the parents. " . . . Read to him a lot. . . . Make sure his eyes move across the page in the proper fashion, from left to right. And hold his hand as he traces the words he reads."

Then the child would be toured around the school once more, by an older brother or sister if he had one. Otherwise, I myself would tour the family around.

<u>The first day</u>

When the child actually started, his mother brought him to school and went into the classroom with him. Then, after perhaps fifteen minutes, she would leave and come to my office. The idea was to pass the child along, from one person taking care of him to the next, and to avoid that awful hiatus. We wanted to prevent any time of abandonment, before the child was ready.

(Oh how I remember! — for myself. School: being alone among strangers. When I remarked on this to Edna, she said:)

Yes, I myself remember, long ago when I began school, we had to cross that great divide by ourselves.

Anyway, on that first day a new child comes to class with his mum. But the teacher couldn't begin the real teaching until the mothers had left the room. The mothers understood this. After awhile, when the child seemed comfortable, his mum might ask, "May I take Teddy shopping?" (They would have probably come to school carrying his Teddy bear.)

(Thinking of America, and my time at school, I naturally thought of teasing by the other children. —Coming to school with your mother, carrying a Teddy bear.)

—Oh no. Certainly not! There never was any teasing.

Anyway, the new mums, after they'd left their children in class, had tea with me in the staff room. And we chatted. The group of new mums was . . . . It was similar to what you would call a support group. The experienced mothers, who already had older children in school, could be helpful to the new mums who were going through this for the first time.

After about half an hour, I took the group of mothers around on a tour of the school. We used to look in through the large windows of the reception class. The children would be busy with whatever they were doing. A few mums might become a bit tearful. Perhaps they were surprised to see their children getting along so well without them.

If there was any child . . . Occasionally we got a child who found it harder to accept school. Then the mother would go into the classroom again, and sit with him longer.

Overall we had very little difficulty, merging them in happily. But for that occasional child: his mother just stayed with him longer.

When it was time for the new children to go home, the mothers reentered the classroom on the teacher's invitation; and they went home with their own children.

. . . I told the parents: I wanted them to walk their child to school, and deliver the child to the teacher; then at the end of the day, take him back again and walk him home. The idea was to pass the child along, from one protective adult to the next. On the playground, one of us might take the child by the hand. I can remember, still: our gruff Deputy Head, holding a new Infant by the hand, touring him around the playground.

(During one of these encounters: little Simon Cramp, on his first view of the schoolgrounds, looked up at him and asked him what was his favorite piano concerto.)

I think that in the beginning, children should be protected. Then when they choose to be independent, they can start doing things on their own.

I had one little boy come to me and say, "Mrs. Ward, I know how to tell time. Would you like for me to go and find out what time it is now?" Of course I was wearing a wristwatch. I said "Yes please." So he did.

Infants

Children start school as rising fives. Some are actually five years old. Others are almost five; and still others, four and a half. In the early years, from age five to seven, they are called Infants. After that they become Juniors, aged seven to eleven.

They begin in a Reception Class. At the end of the first term, at the half-year, the older pupils move on to the next-oldest class. The others remain in the Reception Class for one more term. They, now, become the older and more advanced pupils to the new Infants who are just entering.

And this mixture continues through ensuing grades: older children who will move on at the next change-of-term, and younger children who have just entered the class and who will remain for two terms.

This is advantageous for ability groupings. An older child who is slow in, say, reading, can be grouped with younger children. Since they are all in the same class anyway, he does not feel so embarrassed by this. But it has another advantage too, which I think is even more important. The older children are often doing more advanced work. And the younger children can see this going on around them. They get a preview. When it becomes *their own* work, in the following term, they already are familiar with it.

Sometimes, also, we could combine the two age groups. We might put numbers up. The same numbers might be used for: recognizing and naming the numbers, for the younger children; and addition, for the older children.

The Reception Room

The children come to school that first morning in their school uniforms. They are exceedingly proud of these. They have seen those uniforms on the older children. Now they have a uniform of their own. It is often too big, with the blazer reaching down to the knees. The child will grow into it.

The Reception Room—we tried to make it a comfortable and home-like place. All of the schoolrooms are personalized for the children, with plants, maybe pets, their pictures on the wall. However the beginning children need to be surrounded by extra comforts, and these we endeavored to provide.

We told them they could bring a favorite toy to school, a soft toy. Also they brought their Teddy bears. There was a Wendy house in the Reception Room, which children could retire into. There were two little beds in the Reception Room. A child, if he felt a need to withdraw, could lie down on one of these beds, and another child would cover him up.

It's all especially gentle at first, with a measured pace to the school day. There is a time for having your drink. They have their orange juice or their milk. There is a time for washing one's hands. There is lunch time. They leave their schoolroom and go, together, to the school lunchroom. There, they will sit at table as if they were at home, and an older boy and girl will sit with them, just like their parents would do at home.

There is a time for feeding the school's pets. (Rabbits and guinea pigs). An older child might appear at the Reception Room's door and say, "Anyone want to come help feed the animals?"

The Wendy house was large enough so that two children could get into it. It had tiny chairs and a stove. A new child, if he had a relapse in his confidence, might want to retire into the Wendy house with his toy.

There were always many of the older children, especially the older girls, who were eager to mother the little ones. An older girl might go into the Wendy house with him and try to comfort him.

It intrigued me, how popular the Wendy house was for the little boys. One might suppose that they would think it too girlish to play house. But all that seemed to relax at school. Any pent-up desires to do girlish things, or babyish things—seemed to come out more freely.

Again: no teasing?

Certainly not!

Along with the Teddy bears, we had all the accompanying equipment. The mothers made special clothes for the Teddies. These were usually little school uniforms. We had miniature chairs which were the Teddy chairs. You could have your Teddy sitting next to you. And we kept some spare Teddies. If any child felt especially bereft, and he had not brought his own Teddy, well, we could provide a substitute.

When children were learning to write, we might give them a piece of paper folded down the middle. "Let's write a book for Teddy." —

"This is a cat." —Teddy would be sitting in his little chair, and the book would be placed in his arms.

Children began with these comforting toys, and then they gave them up when they were ready. A child might say, "Teddy didn't want to come to school today."

"— Well that's all right. Teddies don't have to. But we must be here, mustn't we."

Usually they were given up rather quickly; sometimes to be retrieved later, as the need arose.

However there is something special about the Teddy bear.

(During the wartime evacuations of London, Teddies were carried onto the trains.)

I've had Teddies come on the school trip to France.

Very occasionally we got a child who had not yet been parted from her dummy. (Her pacifier). They were discouraged from sucking on the dummy while in class. However they could bring it to school. It was kept for them in a drawer—a secret drawer—in my office. They knew they could repair to my office and have it in their mouth when the need arose. . . . We had one little girl who wanted her dummy with her. So I said, look, there is such a lot of people all together here, and a lot of toys and books, it might get lost. Shall we put it in this special bag here? And I put it in my drawer.

And for several weeks, every morning, she used to bring it to me. . . until, finally, she never bothered to bring it to me.

Weren't you having a lot of interruptions?

I was accessible to the children. So was the staff. We just had to learn to manage with the interruptions. A distressed child was more important than my other work.

When the children could first begin to write just a few words, they would send me notes—pushed under my office door usually—little messages like "How are you?" and "I love you." I would then answer the notes. Their answers would be on their desks the next morning.

Again I marveled at the contrast with my old school in America. All this indulgence! Babyishness certainly would not have been tolerated back there. I remember my first view of that intimidating school playground. Kids were jostling each other. Boys were bumping into other boys. This was a version of King-of-the-Mountain, which was a typical preoccupation of the boys—which boy could make another boy back down. I myself was afraid. I finally got up my courage and approached the smallest, weakest-looking little boy. I bumped him. He punched me right in the nose. I was stunned. That was the end of my bully career. Now I see, I was really meant for Edna's school. But instead I was stranded at my American school, amid this bumping.

When I told this story to Edna, she was amused. She said "I'm afraid we weren't very <u>macho</u> at Mossford Green. Learning to read was the great acclaimed achievement, not prowess at fighting or sports."

<u>Summary</u>

To sum up: Anything like school phobia was avoided. Children came to school with their mothers, were passed on to another adult, then their mothers visited them in their classroom again. There was no great divide to cross—no "hiatus" between protective adults, in which the child was abandoned and alone. Also, by the time they entered the Reception Class they already were well acquainted with the school. They had been visiting, sometimes for years.

Edna says, "We tried to bridge the gap between home and school as gently as possible. We tried to make school an extension of home."

It was tolerated—it was perhaps expected—that new children would occasionally slip back into babyish behavior. Provision was made for this. Little boys, in the Wendy house, could indulge in what was perhaps girlish behavior.

Hearing about all this, I'm thinking: although Edna and the school did some lovely things, still—they had to have the help of the older children—not teasing, not bullying. I myself remember with shame how I treated my little brother. I regarded him as a pest. He always wanted to be included. The older children at school seem to have had the opposite, parental, protective attitude.

Edna: I think the secret to having a happy start in school, more than anything, was the acceptance by the other children. Did they remember from their own experience? —that they themselves had once been new to the school, and they needed help to settle in? The older children were very welcoming. And, as I said, the big girls loved to mother the little ones.

As for myself, long ago, being intimidated by that jostling playground at school—and my son Mark, years later, having the same experience in our hometown—we had no protection on our school playgrounds. There was no supervision by adults. (At least as far as I know there wasn't.) At Mossford Green: not only were the children less aggressive; the adults were watching. There was a teacher assigned to the playground. The dinner ladies helped too. Older children were looking out for the Infants also.

Edna says, if there ever had been anything like an act of bullying, "then half the school would be on him. — 'Oh Mrs. Ward! Arthur pushed Michael! He almost fell over!'"

Bumping, pushing, dominance face-offs between the boys; even competition—a damper had been put on all this.

The same, Edna says, was true for teasing. She doesn't remember any. Maybe somewhere, outside the earshot of the School Head, teasing was not totally unknown. At any rate it seems clear: a damper was put on.

Actually, Edna and the teachers must have been building on a foundation which had been laid by the children's parents. These are somewhat different children from the ones I encountered in my hometown in America—less aggressive, less competitive, milder, softer, more sympathetic, more amenable to school. Edna and her teachers had an easier job.[1] (However see Chapter Six. Several commentators think that Edna would have succeeded, even with more difficult children.)

So the Infants' entry into school could be eased. Was there never a case of school phobia at Mossford Green? — In all her years there, there was one case, a brain-damaged little boy.

<u>Steven</u>

He used to sit at his desk, miserably, with his coat nearby. He would be wearing his gloves and the balaclava helmet he had come in. He would sit with his head down in his arms. He was just suffering it, in utter silence, enduring the day until he would be freed and could go home.

We never attempted to get him to take his balaclava off, or anything else. Some one of us would go and sit by him. Whatever mother was visiting the room, often sat with him. We told her not to urge him to try to do anything.

When it came time to go out onto the playground, the older children, some of them, would come and say "Please may I go and look after Steven?" And they'd take him onto the playground if he would let them. Or they would sit with him. The big girls actually did more with him than the adults did.

The children were allowed two biscuits *(cookies)* at play time. When Steven was sitting there in his gloves and balaclava, you might find half a biscuit, broken off, left next to him. It would have been given by another child.

When it came time for school assembly, Steven's class would go in with the rest. His teacher would bring him in and sit him on her lap, still in his balaclava and gloves.

By the end of the first year he had begun to pick up a pencil. He would sit with his Teddy on a chair near him. And then gradually, gradually, all his extra comforts—his coat, his balaclava—he could dispense with them if they were not put too far away.

When I retired, he was two-thirds of the way through school and he was quite a normal little boy, a slow learner, and shy, but he would speak if you spoke to him.

We had another little boy who was also a slow learner; I might say almost a non-learner. We called him WOL. He too didn't want to come to school in the beginning. When his mother brought him that first morning, he didn't want to enter through the school gate.

I said, "I know what. I need a new helper." So thenceforth I would meet him at the gate in the morning. He would take my briefcase from my hand. And he strode behind me, carrying it, as I walked back to the school.

<u>Mrs. Edna Ward</u>

Edna began her teaching career after the War, at John Bramston Primary School in Ilford, which is suburban to London. She dropped out to stay home with her own daughter, during the little girl's pre-school years. After Edna had returned to teaching, she took charge of Mossford Green, in Ilford, in 1964.

Mossford Green was a fairly new primary school, serving mainly a lower middle-class clientele. It took in three-hundred-fifty children, with up to thirty-nine pupils in a classroom.

This was a period of ferment in British education. Edna was one of the leaders in the national movement toward new, liberalized teaching methods. She served a term as president of the National Head Teachers' Association. However she retired early from Mossford Green, in 1977, to stay home with her husband who was ill— much to the chagrin of parents, teachers, and pupils.

Mossford Green may have been unusual on some points. But in a general way it represented the norm, or perhaps the ideal, for British primary schools in the 1960s and 70s and 80s. Now, as I've said, the schools have gone bureaucratic. We will return, later, to this dismal story.

<u>Note</u>

1. British children and their parents' efforts are described in chapters five and six in our book, *Civility in an English Village.* (Severn Books, 2000. http://www.wstephens.net) For discussion of British parents and their preschool children, the writings of Judy Dunn should also be mentioned. (*The Beginnings of Social Understanding*, 1988, Harvard University Press; and others of her books); and also *Four Years Old in an Urban Community* (London: Allen and Unwin, 1968), by John and Elizabeth Newson.

Chapter 2

THE SCHOOL DAY

Before school, the children could either play outside on the playground; or they went inside and proceeded to their own classrooms. They hung their coats on the coat-pegs, put away their books and other belongings. The teachers would have set out activities-materials on tables: arts and crafts, books . . . After a while the school bell rang; the school day had commenced.

The teachers called the register. Directly, the classes went to the assembly hall—quietly, but not in a queue or crocodile. (*There was almost no lining up or standing in line, in Mossford Green School.*)

<u>Assembly</u>

We all met together at half past nine for morning assembly—everybody in the entire school. A few of the mums would usually come too, and with them a few of the little preschool children. Safety Sam who saw the children across the street, he would come in. There was a hatch which opened from the kitchen, so the cooks were visible from the waist up. They stopped their work and were a part of the assembly also.

I would come in and the children would stand. I'd say, "Good morning, children." They'd say, "Good morning, Mrs. Ward. Good morning, teachers." I'd make my way to the front and I would bid them sit down.

(I inquired about any background noise, giggling, scuffling, smart-aleck behavior.)

Oh no. It was relaxed, very pleasant, but they were all quiet . . As you know, I am unable to raise my voice and speak loudly. And I had no trouble, there, in making myself heard.

We would begin with a simple prayer, and then a hymn. One of the head children would open a window for Mrs. Hemming across the street, so she could hear the singing.

Then if I had any news I would get up and tell them. For example I might describe the display which one of the classes would have put out, that week, in the vestibule of the school.

There was always some kind of display in the vestibule. It might be a shell collection, or other kinds of nature collections. It might be a display that the children themselves had collected, perhaps wildflowers, or flowers they had produced from their gardens, or their art works or crafts, or pottery they had made. Each week, it was one classroom's turn for the vestibule-display. So I might talk about the current display.

If any child had done something particularly noteworthy, maybe written a story, they might come up and read it to the school. If any of the slow readers had finally been able to read his page he had been working on, he would be invited to stand up and read his page. Any child's particular achievement would be announced. This would be done, unless that child didn't want it. Some children were embarrassed by having their awards announced, and didn't want it. That is the way my granddaughter is today; and I myself was that way.

Then any Infant's birthday would be announced. The children would all say, "Happy birthday, Charlie." (Or whomever.) And Charlie would grin. Then one of the older children counted out the sweets for Charlie, out of my sweets jar. One .... two .... three .... four .... for how old Charlie had become on that day. If any of the little ones who were visiting with their mums, were having a birthday too, that would also be announced, with the sweets. Occasionally something amusing would happen; such as, an older child might say, "Mrs. Ward! Stop! He had a birthday already, last month."

It was all very family-like.

Once every week, one of the Junior classes took over the assembly. They would have a theme, something they had been studying, and they might read their poems about it, or enact a little play, or perform a dance they had made up.

Then I would tell a story.

What kind of story?

Sometimes it would be from the lives of the saints, if that day fell on one of the saints' days. Sometimes it would be an animal story. Occasionally there would be some other kind of story. All the stories had a moral. But it would be something that the Infants could understand. It was all very informal. A child might raise her hand, and there might be a question or two.

Then the Infants and the little preschoolers would leave the assembly, and I was left with the Juniors. I would tell them anything I had for them. And we might proceed with the discussion. The older children enjoyed discussing problems of moral choice, and if something of this nature had come up with the story, we might talk about it. Or I might give them another story which invited more grown-up discussion.

I questioned her some more about the children being so attentive and well-behaved. She mentioned, again, her inability to raise her voice in order to be heard. She and the children would practice together, experimenting to see what tiny movement of her finger . . . . "they'd watch me like a hawk" . . . . would be the signal to them, to stand up or sit down, speak or whatever.

Then I asked again about teasing, belittling, the older children laughing at the little ones.

Oh no! The children were so careful about that. The Juniors would never laugh at the Infants.

She told the story of a five-year-old, leaving assembly, who saw her eleven-year-old brother standing there. The little girl rushed to him, flung her arms about him, and kissed him. Nobody laughed. Then she and the other Infants left the room, and there was some laughing afterwards.

Steven, sitting in assembly in his balaclava and gloves, on someone's lap—certainly no one would laugh. Or Peter Nichols, after his mum had died, sitting on a teacher's lap—three hundred or more children sitting in assembly, and one child on an adult's lap.

Anyone who needed cuddling:

We always made it clear, why. We always said, "He needs special attention."

After assembly everyone went back to their classrooms, and the next period was devoted to maths. There was some blackboard teaching—the division of money, counting up to one hundred—that old traditional method of teaching, which we knew so well, blackboard teaching. But we tried to keep this to a minimum. Its purpose was to prepare the children to start work on their own, on their own workbooks and on their own projects. This is what they did, most of that time.

During this period, Mrs. Opposs began setting up her Special Help class, which was held in the teachers' lounge. Children who came for her remedial instruction, would be sitting in the teachers' lunchtime chairs.

Next was Break time. A child could go out on the playground or stay inside. He might want to go back to the arts and crafts tables, and continue with something he had already started on; or go to the library corner; or perhaps do some sewing, or play chess. A teacher was always there in the room with the children, available for help, noticing whatever they were working on.

Playground

The playground surrounded the school on three sides. It was fenced off against the neighbors' back gardens and the busy streets. There, too, a staff member was on duty. A part of the playground was for the Juniors; onto which, Infants might wander if they wished. And another part of the playground was for the Infants.

I would have to include the older children among the helpers on the playground too. They were always coming up to volunteer. "Mrs.

Lumley, may I go help at the Infants' playground?" —Holding the rope for skipping rope; or retrieving balls which had rolled into the bushes; and, just, acting protective.

(She evidently is amused by the scene she has conjured up, and she smiles.)

We had some unusual play materials that had been discarded and donated to us: a boat, some twenty feet long, anchored in concrete; a steamroller that had once been road-work equipment; and two artificial hills, side-by-side, the result of an old construction project.

Many kinds of imaginary play took place. Ropes hung from the hills; mountain climbing took place, and other make-believe dramas. Children crowded into the boat, sat side-by-side on its seats, swaying back and forth in the heavy seas, with perhaps the occasional child being sick over the side. I would call from my window, that looked out onto the playground: "Where are you off to today?" And the answer would come back, Timbuctoo or wherever.

There was a sliding-track on one of the hills, for when there was a bit of snow or ice. There was a complete weather station, with instruments, on the top of one of the hills. We kept daily records; one child being in charge, every day, taking readings. There were also garden patches along one of the fences. A child could have his own garden if he wished. There was a football pitch and a netball pitch, and marked-off places for other games.

Most of the playground was grassed; we called this the field. Some of it was paved, all-weather, fit to be played on all the time. The more interesting activities were mostly on the grassed part; and this part they could not go onto much of the year. Once again, they were so cooperative. We didn't have to police them. They followed the rule. But there was such enthusiasm on a day when they could go onto the grass, go up on the hills, or slide on the sliding path.

There were numerous other instances of this, how cooperative the children were. The wall around the playground was not very tall; and it had a fine broad coping stone at its top, so it was easy to walk along. This they used to do, and that was all right until, finally, a boy fell and was injured. He said the wall wobbled. I realized that some of its stones were coming loose. So I had to ask them, then, not to walk on the wall any more. And they complied.

We always took pains to explain, when we asked the children not to do something. (Or when we, otherwise, changed a rule, or announced a new rule.) Also, so many of the older children were so parental; we asked them to please watch the little ones to see that they didn't do it—not that the little ones were disobedient, but they were young, so they might forget. So, I think, the older children were all the more on our side.

Another example of their cooperativeness was the exhibits in the vestibule. If an exhibit was judged too delicate to handle, then I would draw a chalk line round it. The children couldn't step over the line and touch anything. If I hadn't drawn the chalk line, then someone would ask, "Is this a touching exhibit, or a not-touching?" If it were in fact a not-touching, then a child would get a piece of chalk and draw the line.

Nothing was ever broken.

Also, to go back to the playground, there were the animal hutches. These were in an alcove just outside my office. The older class was in charge, for feeding and cleaning the pens. Those children took turns.

Not only did we keep records from our weather station, we recorded birds which were sighted on the playground, and insects from the playground. We gathered flowers from the playground and put them on display, in school. The playground was very much a part of the school.

The fire escape chute, from the second floor of the building, was a great favorite. They loved it. They would ask, "Will we be having a fire practice soon?"

Once every year we had sports day. There was excited preparation, marking the courses for the events.

Were there prizes and blue ribbons, first place, second place, awards?

No. None. An Infant was awarded a sweet for simply doing all the events. It didn't matter if he came in last in all of them.

Edna told other stories of their relations with the neighbors who lived on the other side of the wall. When two boys put a cricket ball through a neighbor's greenhouse, she went with them, with a bouquet of flowers, to apologize. . . . When a thoughtless neighbor dumped a pile of ashes over the wall, the Infants, in their new school uniforms, discovered it. They assumed it had been left for them to play in. Sometime later they were discovered by older children, and led in, their uniforms hopelessly bedraggled and soiled. . . .
To sum up, two main themes, again: protection for the little ones—by staff who are watching; by Edna, viewing from her window; by dinner ladies at noon; and by the older children themselves. The other theme is: enrichment; school as an exciting place; and playground activities which do not rely on competition to provide interest.

<u>The Crow</u>

We were once terrorized for about a week, by a crow who took up residence on the roof of the school. It was extremely aggressive, like no crow I had ever seen. It would surge down upon the children on the playground, or when they were coming to school. It would peck them on the head, sometimes grab a little girl's hair ribbon, maybe peck at their shoe laces. More than once, its pecks fetched blood. The children would go out onto the playground; crow would spot them and come swooping down; and the whole school would run pell mell back into the building.

During this week the phone line was jammed: distraught parents whose children were afraid to come to school.

One scene I remember: I was standing at my office window with a school inspector, and we were looking out onto the schoolyard. There was a football match in progress. Suddenly—the crow must have spotted them—because he came swooping down. People—children, staff, parents—scattered, rushed back into the building. —Leaving the crow in possession of the field. —But two brave boys stayed on. I can remember them running toward the goal, the crow flying about their heads; and they kicked a goal. And then they finally escaped. The crow was left with only the ball to attack; which he did.

We tried a number of strategems for getting rid of the crow. The children told me that he liked Maltesers. So Dorothy Marx, my secretary, and I—we attempted to trap him in an old rabbit hutch. We had Maltesers inside the hutch, and Maltesers in a trail along the ground, and a string tied to the opened door of the hutch, and—we were very brave—we were tossing Maltesers out to him. And the crow was getting closer and closer to our trap. The school was watching through the windows. But he never entered the trap.

In the end I had to call in the pest control people. They went up on the roof. They reported: he had amassed a great store of stolen goods—shiny wrappers off sweets, hair clips, hair ribbons, anything that was bright.

Anyway, peace was restored.

<u>Workbooks</u>

So—after the break period it was time for English class. In the Infants' classes, they were of course learning how to read. As soon as they could read anything at all, the Infants were reading out loud. They were listened to, individually, by adults. The teacher did this, and also the helper mums. This went on all day, not simply in this English period. Each child read to a grown-up at least three times per week, usually more.

I should say about the helper mums: in the first year of Infants, it was normal that a few mothers would be in the classroom, to give comfort. I left it to them: a mother came until her child seemed ready to be on his own; and he was usually ready very soon. After that, I tried not to have mothers in the same classroom with their own children. It interfered with a full-fledged teaching effort.

At the beginning, I gave the parents a list of things they could do as volunteers, if they wished. But this did not include, assisting in their own child's classroom. A mother might be out in the hallway, hearing reading. Also the parents did little special classes. A mother might be teaching a cookery class. Fathers helped with sports. Parents had crafts groups.

Anyway—meanwhile, during the English class in the Juniors' classrooms, there were the workbooks. The teacher wrote their day's assignment on the blackboard.

Every child had his maths workbook and his English workbook. He would have an assignment, so much every day. After the teacher wrote the assignment, the pupils began. The teacher was there to help and explain. When a child finished he could do something else. And we planned it so that, normally, he would have some extra time.

He might have a book which he wanted to finish. Or he might want to get a book in the school library, for work on some project he was doing, perhaps in geography or in history.

So a child would progress in this fashion, through his workbook, day by day, until he had finished it. When it was finished, it had to be brought to me. The child brought it personally. I went slowly through it, reading, the child looking on. Then I wrote my comment and my signature. The comment would be something simple like "Good work but could you make the next one a bit more tidy?" Then the child took it home to show his parents.

<u>Lunch Period</u>

Those children who didn't go home for lunch, ate in the dining hall. Infants went to lunch first, soon followed by the Juniors. As with everything else, a teacher was in attendance; also there were dinner ladies.

It was official policy in all the schools to serve lunch cafeteria-style. I resisted this. I thought the little ones, especially, needed more of a family setting for their meals; besides, they were too young to make good choices in a cafeteria line. So in our lunch room, an eleven-year-old boy and girl sat, like father and mother, at a dinner table with six Infants. The older children were keen to do this, and so they took turns.

The Italian cook and one or two of her helpers opened the hatch to the kitchen; the older children went up and received the food, in serving bowls (like at home), and took the bowls back to their table. And they commenced serving the children.

They would say, "Would you like some of this cabbage? . . . Just a very little? . . . " (The only rule was: if a child asked for some, he had to make a good try at eating what he received.)

In this way the older children proceeded, serving the Infants at their table, then serving themselves. (*It sounded like a slow method.*) When all were served, then the children at the table could begin eating.

It sounded pretty delayed. I asked if it was hard to get the children to wait like this. She said, oh no, normally they came from homes where this was the custom anyway. Then she said, there might be the occasional child who needed to be restrained or reminded.

But later, we were told about one really flagrant violation of the rule. A boy—now a young man—admitted that he and other older boys, at other tables, had hurried the Infants through so that they themselves could go out and play football during the remainder of the lunch period.

The teacher who was in charge of the lunchroom would sit at an Infant's seat at one of these tables, and the older child would serve her as he would another of the Infants. And the meal would proceed as it would at home. The dinner ladies were there (standing in the background, not at the table). They didn't help with the serving either. They might go help if something were spilled.

The older children found themselves acting like parents. They would cut a child's meat for him, do things of this nature. They made sure each Infant got a chance at everything. If a child said, "I don't like gravy," that was all right. But if a particular child was, repeatedly, not eating very much, then they would consult the teacher.

After the meal was over, the older children carried everyone's dirty dishes and bowls back to the cooks. And they rearranged the chairs and tables again. This they did quickly. They enjoyed it, I think. It was part of running the school. (The dining hall also served as the assembly hall. So the older children had to arrange the chairs and tables for lunch period, beforehand; and then put them back, after lunch.)

The older child who presided at table, never insisted that the Infants eat what they didn't want. —Beyond inquiring at the beginning, if they would try a tiny bit. There was always plenty of food left in the bowls. So he'd say, "Who wants . . . . seconds?" Or: "Would you like a bit more to drink?"

(With a child who wasn't eating:)

The teacher or dinner lady might tell me: Michael isn't eating much at all. So I'd say, all right, I'll phone his mum. And I would; I'd tell her he wasn't eating much. I'd inquire, "Do you want him home for lunch, or will you simply feed him up after he gets home after school?"

As with other things which the Infants did, there were some misunderstandings. And some of these were amusing.

Once, one of the little ones went to the dinner lady, crying. (What's wrong?) The child told her: "He asked me, 'do you want custard or pie or both?'" (So? What was wrong?) . . . "And I didn't know what 'both' was."

Little children do have their quirks; as, for example, not wanting to eat the peas and potatoes on their plate, if the two vegetables have touched each other. And they would be easily brought to tears, in the lunchroom, at first, before they were comfortable with the routine. The older children would have to deal with this.

Really, though, not much supervision was needed. Our Sicilian cook and our French caretaker required more supervision, probably, than did the children at lunch. They had very emotional arguments. They often sounded quite violent, while the children were so mannerly.

After the meal, everyone remained sitting at table until the last child had finished. *(This too sounded like it could be a major delay.)* Then one of the older children asked for the plates; and the plates were stacked at his end of the table. Then he indicated that they could leave the table.

I imagined the children, pent-up, waiting to run out onto the playground. I marveled at the discipline. I asked if some of the older children were unready to play a parental role like this. Were there any exceptions? She couldn't remember any. But then later we got the confession by the older boy. We don't know how many lapses there were. Edna thinks that if any of the older children erred, it was more likely in the opposite direction. Some of the big girls were inclined to smother the little ones with their attentions, and baby them.

Creative Crafts

After lunch, tables were laid out in all the classrooms, for crafts. We had work in clay, painting, sewing, knitting, woodworking, model building, cooking. Joan Lumley did a popular one in batik dying. Stanley Attridge had them crocheting little squares, which then could be put together to make, say, a waistcoat. I did one on toy-making.

Some of these were rather messy. The children dressed in their fathers' old shirts, hanging down to their ankles; or smocks or aprons. So they could be splattery. But they did have to be careful with the crafts materials and not waste them, since these cost money.

Especially for the older children, the scheduling was flexible. A child might leave his room, go to another room, work alongside a friend from another class.

—"May I work in clay today?" And we'd say yes, go down the hall to Mrs. Barnett's room; or to Mr. Griffin's room; and ask if there is room for you in clay modeling (or in whatever it was).

—Flexible up to a point. Once they began, they had to stick with a craft for five or six weeks. Then they could move on. And they did have to move on, eventually. We wanted them to try a number of things.

We had one little boy who always wanted to sew. He made toys and dolls with his sewing. We had a struggle, getting him to do anything else. And perhaps we needn't have bothered. Today he is a Saville Row tailor, making posh suits.

Again, we de-emphasized anything like competition or comparisons between the children. It didn't matter whether you were good or not.

(I am skeptical on this score, that the talented children didn't get special notice; and the especially untalented, perhaps, weren't sometimes embarrassed. But that is what she said.)

Meanwhile, while this was going on throughout the afternoon, Mrs. Opposs was continuing in the teacher's lounge, with Special Help. Also, music teachers were coming in. Every child played recorder; there were lessons in that. And there were small classes for woodwinds, strings, percussion, and brass. Also there was junior orchestra practice. We wanted to make learning an instrument very accessible to the children. The instrument could be rented, very cheap, for the first year.

For myself, I had the toy-making in the afternoon, and a little French class. In addition, during the morning I taught every class in the school, for one period, every week. This gave the teachers a rest period, which they needed. They were doing concentrated hard work. Also, I always managed to visit every class, every day. I loved going round. They'd show me a story they had written or something they were making.

It was never silent in a classroom. There was always a background buzz, a murmur of activity; but never shouting or scuffling or misbehavior.

(Again I was skeptical. But she said this was so.)

We wanted a relaxed atmosphere, with children going around trying new crafts. We tried to have as much happening as possible. It was terribly organized, while seeming to be informal. Something was always going on.

And the children were so cooperative. That made it possible, I know. There was no problem, no disturbance, in children going through the halls, from one room to another. They went by themselves; they didn't need any extra surveillance.

The crafts groups in particular looked so informal, to the point of being disorganized. But the children were so focused on their own individual crafts projects; they were not about to be diverted onto anything else.

How about social studies—history, geography?

That was the last period in the morning, before lunch. I had forgotten about that. It alternated with gym.

(I remarked that this seemed like an easy schedule, English and maths and this other in the morning, nothing but crafts and music in the afternoon.)

On the contrary; we worked flat-out. —The children, the staff, all of us. I loved it, but I was tired at the end of the day. The children worked to the limits of their capacity; and they did very well.

How about special events? You mentioned sports day. There was a picture of the harvest festival. . .

Harvest festival, Christmas performances. . . The children put on plays. There were concerts, separate concerts by the Junior orchestra and by the Infants. The Infants performed on their recorders with great pride. There was much singing of course.

(I had seen pictures of the children dressed up for make-believe, in adults' clothes.)

Yes, that was something the Infants did, in maths class. That was learning to count money. They played shopkeeper and played mums with their market baskets.

Then there were numerous activities that went on at school on their own time, not in class. Taking care of the animals. Clubs: we had a chess club, and a stamps club, and from time to time, other clubs. Sports teams had their practices after school. The school was represented by a football team (soccer) and a cricket club, and netball. I daresay they felt it was an honor to represent their school.

So, there <u>was</u> some competition. It wasn't all noncompetitive.

That's right. The emphasis was on group competition, not competition between individuals. But of course some of that was unavoidable too.

And we had days out. We would hire a coach (a bus) and take the children out to places of interest which tied in with what they were doing at school. We might say: let's see how many ways there are for crossing the Thames. So the coach would take us over historic bridges we had studied, and some we hadn't studied; and under in a tunnel; and over the Tower Bridge that moved. We crossed on a ferry also.

Sometimes the Infants would leave the school on their own trips, perhaps to the park for nature study and gathering specimens; and the Juniors would go on their own, for example to museums in London.

Mr. Pithers, Mr. Gurr, Mr. Eastwell

Also we would have visitors, guest speakers. Somebody's granny might come in and talk about her travels to Australia, when she had been young. Grannies were very popular. The children were terribly proud of their grannies. A group of children would gather round them, and they would talk about what had happened in their lives. They would tell about what Barkingside had been like, before it became absorbed into the city. They would tell about the war, the bombing. That was always popular.

Somebody's grandpa, too, had been the village blacksmith. He came in with pictures of blacksmithing. He talked about shoeing horses. My father-in-law came in and spoke. He had been a master printer. He brought a box of old-fashioned print, letters. He showed them how to put the letters together and print their names.

Several of the neighboring tradesmen were exceedingly generous to the school. They would come in and speak; and they also invited the children to their shops on field trips.

The Eastwells had been an old village family. They were fruiterers, greengrocers. Mr. Eastwell spoke about where the fruits and vegetables came from. Every morning, he said, he got out of bed at three or four o'clock and went down to Covent Garden. Some of the produce, there, which he got for his shop, had been grown under glass in Holland. Some of it had come in from Mediterranean countries. And of course, depending on the time of year, some came from various places in Britain. When the children came to his shop, he might give them carrots, onions, potatoes, or different fruits, to take home.

Mr. Pithers the baker had them into his bakery to see bread being done. Then he came to the school; he brought the proper flour for bread, "strong flour" he called it. The children each made their little cottage loaves. They kneaded their dough, made their loaves, in their classrooms. —I kept the only oven, in my own office, for safety's sake. —Then they would march up the halls, bearing their loaves to be baked, trailing flour onto the floor behind them, and also trailing the ends of their oversized aprons, the daddies' shirt-tails. After the loaves were baked we would display them. A proper cottage loaf had a little knob on top. Then the loaves went home to their mums.

This was considered part of school?

Oh yes. I called it "Environmental Education." That was a new term in those days.

Mr. Gurr the fishmonger also had them to his shop. He took the children down into the stoke hole, where the kippers, mackerel, herring, and haddock were being smoked. It was a rather pungent place. When the children returned, it was obvious where they had ,been. Mr. Gurr would give them a smoked herring wrapped in newspaper, to take home to their mums.

Chapter 3

THE CHILDREN'S WORK AT SCHOOL

We had assessment sheets for each child. They started when the child entered, and continued throughout his school career. They were filled in by the teacher; almost every week she would make entries into them. The parents could see them at any time.

In the beginning, when a child was five or six, we noted such things as the child's ability to talk and express himself; if he was able to be still and pay attention; and social development, how he got along with other children, whether he was at all aggressive or especially nonaggressive. We would note down when he could write his name; when he could write it without copying. . . And maths, similarly: number bonds up to ten (nine plus one, eight plus two . . .) So, in the assessment sheets we had stages: ability to count up to five; counting up to ten; holding the pencil properly; and the like.

During the first few months of a child's career in school, we were finding out what he already knew, how far along he had come in his first four or five years of life. —Learning his colors, buttoning his clothes, recognizing words on the page as a result of his parents having read to him, and so on.

And of course when children begin school, there is such a difference in maturation—simply, in biological development. Some of them are just more matured. Others are not nearly so ready for school.

Then, as far as the assessment sheets are concerned: later, at the Junior level, it got more complicated. We tried to write down something about a child's approach to problems; and something about aesthetic and mechanical and physical abilities and limitations. . . . (For example, a teacher might note on the sheets: "be careful of his balance during gymnastics.") And in exceptional cases, we would say something about the home situation, if we thought that we should take this into account: father died; divorced parents. . . . That sort of notation.

I can see the form now. I would read it over; and the teacher and I would discuss it together. —For each child. Then I would sign it.

With these sheets, we could see the step-wise progress of any child. And children could be compared with each other. Ability groupings could be made from this; although they were hardly necessary for that purpose.

We had parents' meetings all the time. I was forever trying to persuade the parents, not to compare their child with other children; not to attach too much importance to that. —Since as we knew, children progress in different ways. They take spurts of development. I'd try to persuade the parent: If her child doesn't get to the end of his reading book when some other child does, that's all right, try not be too concerned. Don't pressure him to hurry up.

<u>Workbooks</u>

As I've said, they had workbooks in maths and in English, with an assignment every day. Each child's assignment was geared to his ability; so naturally, some pupils got ahead of others and were doing more advanced work.

Actually there were three workbooks, for English, for free composition, and for maths. When a child finished one of these workbooks it was brought to me. I saw every workbook that every child in the school completed. He and I would read through the workbook together. I'd say, "Well, what do you think? Do you think you've made any improvement?" And he'd look at it . . . and make some appropriate comment. At some point I might interject, "My! I wonder what happened on that day!" (Something wrong perhaps.) Finally I would sign it at the end, and make some written comment.

If the workbook was good enough, it would be sent home for the parents to see, and I would get out my jar of sweets which I kept in my office. —That is to say, good enough, considering which child it was. Did the workbook represent sufficient effort; did it show progress?

That jar of sweets again.

. . . . and give the child a sweet. Yes. The sweets were Smarties.

Did you always tell them the workbook was good?

No, sometimes, after we had gone through the workbook, I would say, "Well, I don't think we should send that one home right now. Your parents might be a bit disappointed."

(1 wondered what else the child might do, to earn sweets out of her sweets jar. Could children earn sweets for good behavior? Or earn something like a gold star?)

No. It was simply assumed that everyone's behavior would be proper at all times. Nearly always, that was the case. Sweets were given occasionally for their work. And at birthdays, as I've said.

It was a personal matter between the two of us, the workbook. Sometimes they would pass me in the hallway perhaps, and say, proudly, "It's almost done! It's good!"

. . . . And of course, between them and the teacher, too, who was looking at their workbook every day; and between them and their parents.

A child who has tried hard with a piece of work hates for you to write on it and . . . . . improve it, cross anything out, make notes in the margin, correct his spelling. If I had said, "Well I think what you have written is lovely. And I hope you had made it a bit more tidy." —The child might say, "You won't spoil it, will you?" (By writing on it.) "But could I borrow your rubber to rub that little bit out, just there . . . " wanting to take it home, perfect.

Ability groupings

Most of the time the children were proceeding on their own, on these workbooks; and then in the afternoons they were doing their crafts too. Then there were some group projects also, preparing for performances and displays and the like. As a prelude to all this, the teacher would do chalk-and-talk, to explain what they had to do. But there was not too much of this.

I might say, too: we always wanted to have plenty of materials, conveniently at hand—the pencils sharpened, paints, glue, everything, fresh pieces of paper . . . We didn't bother about wasting the paper. They could have all they wanted.

(When we visited a village school, Saint Gabriel's, the children were seated at tables of about four or five. They were preparing a group project. A table I sat with, was definitely the slower pupils. The tables looked like ability-groupings to me.)

. . . .

Did you have anything like ability-groupings or streaming at Mossford Green School?

Streaming? —Definitely not! I think that is an insult to a child—to put him in the less-good class. However ability-grouping of some kind is hard to avoid.

But then ability-groups can be different from streaming. The children can all proceed along together, in the same class. And a particular child might be in a slow ability-group for one project, or one subject; and a not-so-slow one, for another. Also, to some extent, we could hide the ability-groups.

It would be deadening, everyone going along at lock-step, studying the same thing, the bright students being held back for the slow ones.

(I know. It _was_ deadening. That is what we had done at the school I had gone to, and chalk-and-talk too.)

The brighter children have to be free to proceed at more or less their own pace. They should be challenged. We couldn't let them sit and get bored. On the other hand, we had to protect the slower pupils. We didn't want to pressure them unduly. We took pains not to embarrass them.

It is obvious in any class, who the bright pupils are, and who the slow pupils are. That is to say, bright and slow, academically. So our problem was: we had to have some sort of ability-grouping. But we had to do it as subtlely as possible. We didn't want to discourage the slow pupils.

We capitalized on two things. First of all, since any classroom had within it, children in an age-range, with some of them being almost a year older than others; and those older ones moving on into the next class at the end of the term; while the younger ones would remain in the same class at the end of that term, and become the older children in that classroom—since we had that, we could do this. When we ability-grouped, we could put slower older children with brighter younger children. This didn't seem to embarrass anybody, as far as we could tell; and it took care of part of the ability grouping that we needed to do.

Also, when we had to divide them into work-groups, with some groups being more advanced than others, we could do this. We'd tell them, "For this group project, you might want to choose another person whom you especially enjoy working with." And ninety-nine percent of the time, they would sort themselves into ability groups. You could then make the few adjustments that needed making. The teacher could say, "Well that's pretty good. But this group over here needs another person. Allan, would you go over there and be with them?"

Another thing that helped was, although bright pupils were usually good at everything, and poor pupils usually bad at everything, there were some exceptions too. We did have the occasional child who might be brilliant at maths but not good at writing. So that also made what we had to do, even less obvious.

And to compensate even more: poor pupils did, sometimes, have their moments of glory. For example Allan Kenton, who was so brilliant at sewing, and made toys and dolls which were so admired—he was a very slow pupil in other respects. A few others of the slow pupils might have some particular gift, in art perhaps, or handwriting, calligraphy. When the children were doing a group project, and it was almost finished, they might say, "Mary, would you do the writing on the cover of the book?"

(And I remembered: A confused little boy whom I had sat with, at the village school, later starred in a school concert.)

. . . .

This manner of teaching, with perhaps six separate ability groups in a class of thirty pupils, working along at different levels, doing slightly different assignments—or with one group at a later part of a sequence, ahead of the others—this demanded a lot of the teacher. She had to be nimble, going from one to the other, perhaps using the blackboard for one group while not disturbing the other groups. . . . She might say to a particular group, "If you would just turn your chairs around toward the blackboard for a moment . . . " and she would explain something to them. Then they would turn their chairs around again and go to work.

Another thing which took an enormous amount of time, was the individual workbooks. If you shift the emphasis, from the entire class sitting and listening to the teacher, to the children working on their own, then naturally that multiplies the teacher's work. Not only did she have to keep track of what each child was doing—look at the workbook, help him when he needed it—and do this fairly frequently, give the child sufficient attention. She had to evaluate the workbooks and mark them also. And this was not so simple, either, because the children would be working at different levels. She had to be aware of signs of improvements, and what a particular child should be *expected* to do.

Our flexible system, in the school, was demanding in other ways. —Our scheduling which was so changeable, with special things being squeezed in, differently, on different days. The welcoming of visitors, outsiders, parents, into the school, and attending to them. Having things be more informal, less regimented, meant more effort. But, mainly, it was the extra work the teacher had to do, when she gave up whole-class teaching in favor of workbooks and ability-groups.

(Whole-class teaching has recently staged a comeback in Britain. The argument in its favor is: the other method of individualized instruction is too difficult; with optimal conditions, the best schools and teachers, perhaps small classes, it can work. Otherwise the teacher tends

to lose track of some of the pupils and they don't make the desired progress.

Needless to say, many possible combinations are possible, teaching the class as a whole part of the time; letting individuals or small groups proceed on their own, part of the time. The question is: which method is emphasized?

If individualized instruction is too hard, the counter-measure would be more teachers or smaller classes.)

Were you able to give the teachers classroom helpers?

<u>Introducing parents into the school as teachers' helpers</u>

Yes. Finally. I brought in parent-volunteers. Nobody wanted that at first. Schools tend to be terrified of parents in the school. I suppose they are afraid the parents would see things, and then make some complaints; say damaging things. *None* of our teachers wanted it. I finally said: all right, we are going to try it anyway, for one term. Then we will decide together, what to do about this, whether we will continue.

So the parent-volunteers came in. We were careful never to have them teaching in the same classroom with their own child. Even then, my greatest fear was that a mother would say something about somebody else's child, that would be hurtful. Anyway, the helper-mums were a great success. After we tried them for that one term, the teachers wanted *more* of them.

So that is what we did. However there are just certain limited tasks which you can ask a volunteer such as that to do. The teachers still had a great load of work.

<u>Slow learners</u>

(Talking about the slow pupils again:) They were never held back and not promoted. That would have been the ultimate insult. Even the slowest pupils, like WOL, were promoted. We'd just keep on working with the child individually, trying to teach him to read. —A forlorn hope in WOL's case.

As I believe I've said, the slow pupils were never teased. Really, the other children were very kind.

37

(A pupil such as WOL or Donald Morris seems to have become a sort of class pet. On Donald Morris:)

He was just odd. He had many fears. When someone flushed the toilet upstairs, and it rattled through the pipes—*that* gave him a start. And he was very slow. About the only thing he learned, with us, was how to get along with the other children. One of them might say, "Mrs. Lumley (or whoever the teacher was), I've finished my work. May I go help Donald now?"

Donald Morris, unable to get some simple point, so that the teacher finally throws up her hands. To the class at large she says: "I cannot think of how else to explain it. Can anyone explain this to Donald?" . . . A little girl's hand shoots up. "Donald, you know when . . . . " And Donald finally, after the little girl's childishly illogical explanation: " . . . . . Oh! . . . . Oh yes. You mean . . . . . ? Oh yes, I see!"

But, amazingly, Donald turned out to be a late-developer. In high school he got an award for academic improvement! I couldn't believe it. And he went on to become a London taxi driver. That would be a very demanding job. Taxi drivers have to pass examinations. And he had to become good at counting money. —Not to mention finding his way around the city. I believe he became a taxi-owner.

We rejoiced together in the occasional successes of the slower pupils. When a poor reader was finally able to read his page, which had been given to him to read some time ago, he was invited to read it to all of us, in assembly. As he struggled along, getting stuck perhaps on particular words here and there, say for example on the word "donkey," one could see throughout the audience the faces straining, the lips moving, the whispered " . . . donkey . . . "

I think it is impossible to totally protect a poor student, all the time. Comparisons are unavoidable. Those occasions will come up, when a child can compare his performance against others', and realize that he is one of the worst. —Worst at that particular thing, at any rate. Everybody knows—you can't stop people from knowing—who the best students are, and who are the worst. What you *can* stop is: people attaching too much importance to it. No one need laugh when Donald Morris couldn't understand the simplest thing. And no one did.

Outside the classroom too, we would cheer for the worst ones. For example we took the children to the swimming baths for lessons. We wanted to get absolutely everybody to the stage where they could swim. There were always several who couldn't do it. When everybody else had passed the test—swimming across the pool or something of that nature—and the non-swimmers were trying it again, the other children would be standing at the edge of the pool, shouting encouragement. "Come on, Richard, swim just three more strokes! You're almost there!" And cheers would go up when they finished.

WOL

. . . . a little scrap of a boy . . . He came from a gorgeous family. Gorgeous! Every weekend they took the children out, on an outing to Epping Forest or . . . (some other enriching experience). When he was having trouble in the beginning, I wrote a note to his mother, asking her to come in and talk to me, to see if we could help John with his reading. She came in on the appointed day, and sat down in the chair in front of my desk, and she said in a slow voice, "Mrs. Ward, I don't know why John is having a hard time . . ." And it was immediately apparent why he was. I think several members of that family were slow. She herself couldn't read. Sometime later, I asked her if she would like to come in privately for reading lessons. She said yes. Ultimately there were about six of the mums who came in.

Who were their teachers?

I was, and sometimes Brenda. (another member of staff)
How well I remember him coming in . . . He loved Pooh books; he would draw pictures of WOL, but I don't believe he ever learned to spell the owl's name.
One time at end-of-term when I had a crowded day, and I kept getting interruptions in my office, I had told my secretary not to let anyone else in. However WOL slipped by. He appeared at my door. I

said resignedly, "all right come in." He came up to me and laid his cheek next to mine, and said sympathetically, "Are you having a bad day?" I said yes I was. He said he was too; "She marked all my sums wrong again." So of course I sympathized. I told him to bring his paper in, and we would try together to set them right.

Special help
       Throughout the day, Special Help was going on, about six pupils at a time, sitting in the chairs in the teachers' lounge, Mrs. Opposs presiding. She was magic! Occasionally I would hear lovely peals of laughter coming out of the room. That would be when one of them made an amusing mistake. They were reading out loud. They were being taught within hearing of the others, and they didn't seem to be embarrassed at all. Quite the contrary. Sitting in those chairs, getting the attention of Mrs. Opposs, was probably prestigious. Children *wanted* to go to Special Help.
       ("May I go get special help in geography?" —"But you don't *need* special help in geography.")
       ("May I go to Special Help? I can't do long division.")
       One little boy, Brian, when he was about eight, said "Oh Mrs. Ward, I'll never be any good at maths. I think I'll give it up and just concentrate on writing instead." And we said, "But you can't give it up. Would you like to go to Special Help instead?" —"Oh yes!" And from the rest of the class: groans, "oh, he's the lucky one!"

       It sounds as if sometimes children sent <u>themselves</u> to Special Help.

       Oh yes. You mean, they simply wanted to go; they didn't really need it. And their decision would be honored. They might go for a couple of days. Then Mrs. Opposs would say how well they were doing. She would say, "You are doing so well, I don't think you need Special Help any more." And the child would agree and return to class.

But there were some children, too, who were actually sent to Special Help?

Yes of course. We all knew who they were, the ones who really needed remedial teaching.

Lillian Opposs was truly desirous that every one of those children get better, and not lag behind, and not be embarrassed about their work. She had a special knack, of giving attention . . . (and perhaps with some flattery, seducing the child into trying harder and attending more closely). So finally the child would read his assignment to her, and she would say: "David! That is excellent! Go to Mrs. Ward and read that passage in just that way!" So the child would come to find me, and probably interrupt me at whatever I was doing. —Radiant with pride, he would read it to me. And I would compliment what he had done.

Some children elected to go to Special Help during the crafts period in the afternoon. It was a pleasant sojourn. She often served orangeade. And they got that wonderful special attention.

However in the *bona fide* cases, it was genuine learning disabilities that we were dealing with. . . .

Knowledge of dyslexia was not so advanced at that time. However we knew that each of these children was doing something in his mind, transposing letters, reading backwards, something. What they were doing, their trouble, was individualized; each dyslexic child was different. It was our job to find the format, discover the individualized pattern, for any child who couldn't read or write. It was detective work. She was good at it. We had one notable failure, only one. Albert Mott. We never found the formula with him—just what was happening in Albert Mott's mind, so that he could not recognize, for example, his name, when it was written out.

<u>Academic results</u>
(I had asked her, at different times and in different ways, how she thought it had all turned out.)

The children compared well in their examination scores. Also, when they went on into high school, the headmaster of the grammar school which got our children—he was very complimentary. He spoke especially of their attitude, their enjoyment of their work. But, he said, could we please teach them to spell? —We had been under-emphasizing phonics, favoring the look-and-say method, so that it showed up in their spelling. So then we tried to set that right.

Another elementary school, Park Hill, also sent its pupils to this grammar school. I think they did equally well. And their examination scores were just as good as ours. Park Hill was formal in its style—to the point of regimentation—the opposite of our informal, flexible style, with all our crafts and optional activities. So either method evidently produced high-performing pupils. I like to think that our school was easier on the slow students.

Also, my desire was not *merely* to produce good students. The school—we tried to create—it was a way of being together. We were giving them an experience of that too.

(In other words, it was a demonstration of a way to live.)

I don't really know how well we did. We had our brilliant students, like Leslie Silver and Stephen Holmes, who went on to Cambridge and to Oxford, and to professorships and great careers afterwards. Aside from those few particularly conspicuous ones—afterwards, as the years passed, I did hear from a lot of the former pupils, and from their parents. I heard many nice things about them; including some of those slow ones, like what happened to Donald Morris. But of course any disaffected pupils, or parents, I would be unlikely to hear from.

They've sent me pictures of their new babies, and of their families. And Christmas cards. That has been such a burden, over the years. *(She smiles and shakes her head.)* Both a joy and a burden. I still get over two hundred, and I must answer.

I still hear from some of the parents too. . . . Particularly during my younger days, we were all parents together, sharing the same experience, going through the same thing. So there still is a bit of that, news of grandchildren and the like.

<u>The parents</u>
(This feeling of collegiality certainly comes through, in our recent talks with the parents.)

The parents were so much a part of it. They brought their children to school, in the beginning. They came to assemblies with their preschoolers and their Infants. Some of them helped in the school. They came to so many parents' meetings. They received the report-books on their children, and responded to what the teachers had written. . . . .

(These report-books differed from the report cards I remember from my school, in that there were no grades or marks. The teachers simply wrote comments in the books, for the parents to read. And a parent could enter her comments also. Then these, with the assessment sheets, could be gone over in parent-meetings, if a parent wished.)

With all that they did for us—teaching crafts, helping in the classroom, helping with trips and sports, the Board of Governors, the parents' association—the most important thing, I think, was with the motivation of the child. A pupil brought his work-book home to show his mum. The parents' appreciation for what their children had done—the children's desire to please their parents with their work—this was crucial, I think. And it could be abused. With a few families it could be a problem.

There were the neglectful parents, who felt that it was all the job of the school, and who didn't help enough in, say, reading with their young children at home. I cannot remember very many of these . . . Anyway, they were less of a problem than the other kind, the opposite extreme—parents who were pressuring their children.

There really is a rather subtle difference between—a parent being interested and helpful—and pressuring. . . .

43

(Yes. I thought of a mother I know, who helps with her child's homework—which is fine—but every night. And three hours a night, maybe more. And I think of parents who help with homework, and their children who produce suspiciously adult-looking papers. I remember a story Edna told about a father at her school, who wanted his son to avoid non-<u>macho</u> activities such as most crafts, and concentrate on football and maths.)

What we wanted was for a child to be working along at a happy pace, for him. We didn't want him to be working anxiously.

(Yes. I remember my youngest son's first-grade teacher, who gave out more work than he could finish. He was always hurrying, often unfinished. It took him some years to get over this—hurrying his work, making careless mistakes, being in a hurry.)

What we didn't want was: for the child's pace of work to be forced, artificially. That interfered with the happy, interested style of work, which was what we were after.

That kind of problem with a parent—one way it might show up, early on, was—the Infants would take their reading book home, with a note from the teacher which might say something like "read to page seventeen." Such a parent might have him reading on, maybe reading the entire book. But after page seventeen there were new words which the child didn't know, words he might not be ready for yet.

The parents' concern about their children and how well they were doing—it was a delicate matter. If a parent found out that another child was ahead of her own—I could understand how, at first, that might be worrisome. My concern about the parent-volunteers helping at school was that those fears would be inflamed. They would make comparisons. I'd try to persuade a parent, as diplomatically as I could, to encourage her child; that's fine, he needs that. But let him develop naturally.

What we were trying to do in the school, depended on the parents understanding this, and cooperating. Most did, well enough, I think. But there were always a few. . . .

(She went on to describe other possible distortions. One is, the parent who says: "I know he doesn't pay attention for very long; but he will if you make him."—Ignoring the child's natural attention span, the product of his stage of maturation.)

<u>Minor tricks of the trade</u>

(In this account we have described the overall outlines of the school. We've left out the many little things which, taken together, add up to quite a lot. Mossford Green had these; other schools, other teachers, have invented their own. Here is one example:)

When the maths class had been going on for long enough, and the children were getting fidgety, we might say: "Enough of this. Go skip your seven-times table." And they would do jump-rope, or they would hop, or skip, while going up a multiplication table. When a child made a mistake, he had to go back to the beginning—that was the game.

Her daily visit to each classroom.

Infants 'shopping,' in queue, learning money values, subtraction and addition.

Crafts.

School pets.

Chalk lines had been drawn in preparation for Sports Day.

Chapter 4

DISCIPLINE

You' ve spoken of how "cooperative" the children were . Was there <u>ever</u> any trouble?

. . . .

Very occasionally. We had the isolated cases. You have to remember, these were very well-behaved children. That was the way they came to us. We just had to continue it.

I know that not <u>all</u> the children came to you, well-behaved. There were the Barnardo's children. There were little boys like Matt.

Occasionally the teacher had to deal with something.

There must have been the occasional noisy classroom. Background noise, whispering, background turbulence, so that the teacher had a hard time being heard.

I only remember that in the case of an occasional child—never the entire classroom. . . .

Several of the student teachers did sometimes permit an unacceptable level of noise in their classrooms. That was an important distinction which I wanted them to learn. There was noise which was acceptable: a certain amount of talking and other noise, even children moving around, when the children were working. That was good. Then there was unacceptable classroom noise. The student teachers had to learn to know the difference.

. . . .

As for myself, the children and I even used to show off a bit, for school inspectors and other dignitaries who came to the school. We had the finger game.

In the beginning, I had said to an assembly-full of children: let's see how small a movement I can make, and you can recognize it, and become silent. So we started with me saying "quiet, now," and moving my arm; and then with me not saying anything, just making an arm movement; then only a hand movement. And we finally got it down to me just crooking the end of my finger. . . . .

We might have a fairly noisy gathering, with me up front. And at some point I would crook my finger—the children would have actually been watching me—and all would fall silent. Instantly. The visitors might ask, "What happened? How did you do that?" But we never told. . . . . .

(In addition to background noise, another issue with keeping order in American schools, is the struggle for control of the classroom. It might begin with one or several children doing something silly—maybe something insolent—to get the other children to laugh. This sort of misbehavior was popular with the children I myself started school with. And it is not unknown in British schools. I asked about this.)

Oh no. The other children wouldn't laugh.

Attention-getting of this nature wouldn't get any approval from the rest of the class. It would meet *dis*approval instead. There were the unusual children such as Matt who tried this. And the other children were frustrated because it interfered with them doing their work. They were angry.

So the attention-getter didn't get anywhere.
How about backtalk? —A child like Matt giving you backtalk.

(She frowned.) Not for me. You have to remember, it has been a long time since I retired . . . Perhaps I have forgotten. But I honestly cannot remember any. I know what you mean by the term "backtalk."

How about the other teachers getting backtalk?

Oh no. I very much doubt that there was ever anything like that. Leslie Silver, the rude note he wrote to one of the other teachers, would have come the closest.

How about Matt?

No, I don't think so. Not even him.

How about scuffling? Roughhousing. Fighting. Anything physical?
(At first she couldn't remember. Then she said:)

Yes, there must have been some kind of incident. I remember calling the entire school in, one time. I put on my most stern manner and I told them, "I want you to know there will be *no fighting* in this school. *Never.*" One of the little Barnardo's boys piped up: "Not even a friendly bundle?" . . . . . Those little boys would have loved to do that, I suppose; tumble about on the floor.

(Years after that, when we were talking to Simon Cramp, he reminisced about having a rock-throwing fight, off the school grounds, with Mitchell and another boy. Word of it had never gotten back to the school, "because we knew that Mrs. Ward hated fighting so.")

This rule—absolutely no fighting on the school grounds—was so ingrained that one time, a dinner lady brought in a girl, Melanie. She said that she had seen Melanie just outside the school gate, and she was shaking her little brother. I said "Melanie! You *know* you're never supposed to do anything like that in the school." And Melanie answered yes, she knew. That's why she had taken him outside the school gate. "The way he was behaving, I was sure he was going to disgrace me." (in the school).
(Then Edna told the story of Anne.) She was a little fat Welsh girl. She pinched other children; and she tried to take their lunches, and she said mean things. Anne became so unpopular that other children might

say, "Oh go away, fatty." When I understood what was happening—Anne's father had come in and complained—I did intervene. The meanness of this situation was so unusual, so atypical.

We never touched a child. We didn't have to.

Oh no. *(She smiles.)* That's wrong. Once I took the cane to Leslie Silver. *(And she smiles again.)*

Leslie was a brilliant student and I was very fond of him. He got along well with everyone except one particular teacher. One day this teacher indignantly showed me a note Leslie had written, which said, very simply, "Mr. (X) is stupid." He demanded that Leslie be caned—totally against our tradition. I didn't know what to do. It was a very unusual offense. Finally I agreed. But only if I myself wielded the cane; and privately, in my office. The teacher demanded to witness the caning, but I wouldn't let him.

At the appointed time, Leslie entered my office, the door closed, I lifted the cane, and there was a great clatter. I had accidentally knocked over a pile of paint boxes with the cane. And I had given him a little tap.

Leslie was never rude to that teacher again.

Years later, when Leslie was a scholar at Cambridge, and we were visiting together, he said that this had been so painful, so embarrassing, that he never ever wanted anything like that to happen again. "It was so undignified both for you and for me, I would never have done it again."

. . . .

We told the children to come to us immediately if another child was interfering with them. This went for bullying—although Anne is as close to a bully as we ever had—or for, simply, another child interfering with you while you were trying to work in the classroom.

When a child was sent to the Head's office because he was being disruptive in the classroom—that is to say, when he was sent down to me—that's all it was, usually. The children at a work-table would complain to their teacher that "Rupert was messing around." —that he wasn't doing his share on their group project; or that he wasn't working and he was interfering with *them* doing their work. This is what a disruptive child was, in most cases. So the teacher would remove him from the classroom and send him down to me. Even children like this, the disruptive children—we trusted them. We did not have anything like hall monitors. They would come to me, bringing their schoolwork. I would sit them in my office, or outside my door in the hall at a little table, and they would do their work for the day. I didn't have to scold them. There was no punishment other than this.

(This hardly sounds like punishment. The child got to be with Edna. Sometimes she even gave him something more interesting to do. Was it embarrassing for them to be called out of the room? —Perhaps, we don't know.)

Chris Reeve, the vicar's son—he was another boy who used to be sent down to me. . . . . . I had a box of foreign coins from our trips to Europe. If they finished their work, I gave them these. And I'd give them a conversion table and say something like "Find all the German coins and see what they are worth in Dutch guilders." I think what happened with Chris was: he decided coming to me and doing what I gave him, was more interesting than staying in the classroom. He would ask for the coins to play with in his free time. *(Note: her trusting of the children with the money.)* . . . . So the coins got too popular.)

(She told stories about children who were sent to her office. Here is one about Rupert .)

He was a beautiful little boy, but he did tend to get in trouble in the classroom. Once I was touring a school inspector around the grounds; and when we returned to my office, there was Rupert, sitting there, downcast. I said "Rupert! Not again!" He hung his head. I said, "What are we going to do with you?"
. . . . . . He finally said, "May I kiss you?"
I said: "Do you think that will make a difference?"
"Yes. Yes." from Rupert.
So I said "Well then bring all your work to me at the end of the day and we'll see if it made a difference."

I stooped and turned my cheek to him. He leaned and gave me a chaste little peck. —All this, with the school inspector looking on. —And it seemed to work. Rupert returned to class and was fine for the remainder of the day. And he did his work.

I asked her what else was done for punishment.

. . . . . . Punishment. . . . . Well there was that: the child being sent to my office. But that was hardly punishment. And—if a child went through the day and didn't do his work, he would have to stay until the day's assignment was done. He couldn't go out on the playground when the others did; he had to stay and do his work. He couldn't do any of the optional activities. He could eat lunch at lunch-time of course. When the school day was over, however, he was kept until he finished his work. The parents understood this.

How about a slow learner like WOL?

He would be given an appropriate assignment at the beginning of the day. —Short enough, so that he should be able to finish and still have some time for himself.

Did anything like scoldings take place?

We did speak to the children when they had done wrong. If they were really naughty, then we told them that we were disappointed in them. Being the well brought-up children that they were, they were vulnerable to this. It was easy to make them very conscious that they'd done something wrong. In other words, you could appeal to their conscience.

I know there are children who are insolent, who cannot be reached. We had the occasional one, I think, who was invulnerable in this way. (Matt.) However . . . .

(And she told some stories: when the football team went on a shoplifting spree; and more.)

Since I cannot raise my voice, I couldn't have shouted at the children, even if I had wanted to. But once I did. It was during assembly. They were excited because it was the Christmas season. There was to be a concert and I was giving instructions of some kind. Right at the back of the room, I spotted a bigger boy, pushing a smaller boy off a bench. I shouted—for me it was a shout—"No!"

There was a shocked silence. The children were aghast. One Infant in the front, began to sob. I apologized to the children. I said I hadn't meant to shout at them. It was only for the one boy at the back.

As I say, they were susceptible. And our entire way of being together, was gentle. You frequently saw a child with a teacher, hand-in-hand. Out on the playground, whoever was in charge, often was going about hand-in-hand with a child. When the Infants came into the school in the beginning—as I've said—they were toured about, hand-in-hand. When a child came to me in my office: I'd hear the tap on the door, and then the child would come in, and maybe lean up against me, so that it was natural to put my arm about him.

(I asked her once more about how they punished.)

. . . . . . There was one other punishment; and it held, like the Law of the Meads and the Persians. If a child did something wrong, and then did it again—then he could not represent the school in competition with other schools, in netball, football, or rounders. This happened rarely, but it was a great blow to the child when it did happen. As I say, it was an honour to wear the uniform and represent the school.

. . . .

For young children, up to about age twelve or thirteen, you do not need punishment. They are so interested in the world—the world is opening up to them, there are so many new things for them—it is easy to interest them. It's easy to manage without punishment, if you don't fob them off with rubbish.

(That is to say, if children are working at projects that interest them, and are not bored by busywork or by excessive chalk-and-talk, then discipline takes care of itself.)

Young teachers, fresh out of college, had to learn for themselves, the ways of keeping children occupied. —How to keep it all moving along. When children like Rupert were sent to my office: sometimes, I daresay, it was because the teacher—at that moment, and for that child—lacked the skill.

It was lovely. —But hard work as I say, both for us and for the children. However almost every night when I went home, I had some delightful story to tell.

The overall system of control

I think it depended on about three elements.

First, there was a code of civility: no teasing, no bullying, consideration for the weak. Competition was de-emphasized. Older children were expected to be like parents to the little ones; as were the teachers.

Second, the children were working on projects they were interested in. As Edna said, "We tried to make the day—their work—so interesting and varied that people had better things to do" (than get into trouble). It was a flexible system, but not "free." Children were not allowed to drift about at loose ends.

Judith, Edna's daughter, is a teacher herself. She is especially talented at working with badly-behaved children. She says this about her own methods: You want to define the children as good, capable, charming; never bad. If possible you ignore provocative acts. You never call attention to them by getting angry or by punishing. And you set in motion some activity that is interesting—something that is intriguing to the children.

Edna's own version of this, held for Mossford Green.

A third element in the system of control was the parents' contribution. Their children were prepared to come to school. They were interested, able to work quietly, capable of self control. The children were grounded in civility; and they were susceptible to appeals to conscience.

Not only did the parents lay the groundwork; they continued to be very much involved. They came to the frequent conferences. The children proudly showed them their workbooks; the children's motivation, at school, hinged partly on this.

I said to her:

That's all right for your regular pupils who got a good start, right from the beginning. But how about that occasional child who did not get a good start? There must have been some *parents who did* not *prepare their children so well, for school. Also, how about someone who transferred in from another school? How about the Barnardo's children? What had their previous school experience been like?*

—Dreadful.

It's true, in cases of that nature, it didn't work so well at first. But they gradually fitted in. I think the tone had been set; the overall ethos of the school was strong enough to overcome influences such as that. But it's true, we did have a very small bit of trouble. And we did have the occasional naughty child, who never did fit in too well.

One sort of child I'm thinking of, who might be expected to start trouble, is a child who got a poor start at the beginning of his time in school. He couldn't keep up. Maybe he couldn't learn how to read at first. You might expect that he would be embarrassed, humiliated; and that he would be bored; so that he wouldn't want to go along, and he might cause trouble. I think this sort of thing happens, many times, in American schools.

I believe we overcame that. Really far-behind children, such as WOL and Donald Morris and dyslexic children: the teachers and the other children were so kind to them; I don't think they were humiliated. In fact they got special attention. And I don't think they were bored. There were other interesting activities for them, at school. I think they still liked school. So they weren't disruptive.

How about hyperactive children? How about little boys who couldn't sit still or pay attention?

. . . . . Attention span. . . . The child with a two-minute attention span. . . . We had a myriad of ways for dealing with that. We all made notes on the children's attention span. One reason I taught every class, every week, was so that I could keep abreast of each child's progress with such matters as that. And one reason for me reading stories in assembly every day, was to demonstrate to the children, just how long their attention span could be.

When a child who we knew had a problem, was beginning to get fidgety, we would try to give him relief. I might say, "David, would you look in that drawer over there? There are some pictures of trees and . . . Would you please look at them and pick out the ones that. . . . "

One benefit to us that the helper-mums provided, was giving relief to a fidgety child. A teacher might say, "Hillary, you haven't had a go at making scones with Mrs. Sharrock this term. Would you like to go down now and make some scones?"

I then asked again: weren't there any children at all, who wanted to hit or hurt other children?

<u>Children who were not amenable</u>
She then cast her mind back over the years, trying to remember other cases.

Matt. He was constantly in trouble. I cannot remember anyone else like him. I don't believe we ever had any success with him at all. He had transferred in from a very tough West Ham school. And he had been spoiled by his parents. He used to be sent to my office almost daily. He would interfere with the other children, steal the colored pencils they were using, break the tips off the pencils, tear pages out of the books they were supposed to use for their projects, hide or steal other materials they needed for their work. . . . I think what must have happened was: first he tried silly pranks; and then when the other children wouldn't laugh, and wouldn't be distracted, he did meaner things such as this. And he did even meaner things. He stole; and he got a mentally-slow little boy implicated in his thefts.

Was Matt physically a bully? Did he hit other children or tussle with them?

No. . . . I don't ever remember anything like that. The complaints about him were different. . . . . What I had said about the children being susceptible to appeals to conscience: Matt would be an exception. I don't think you could reach him. We never could. We never really learned a way to manage him.

He was very bright. That made him even more formidable as a prankster. He could play the trumpet like an angel . . . Another unusual thing about Matt was: his parents wouldn't cooperate with me. They would never come in when I asked. Finally, when I practically forced the father to come to the school, and I told him about Matt's latest provocation, he smiled and said, "Ah that's my Mattie. He'll never be short of a bob or two."

When Matt left us for the high school, later their Head told me about the fire in the school which Matt had set. I don't know what happened to him after that.

Another little boy, Mitchell, might have been similar to Matt. But his behavior was unobjectionable after awhile. I think we didn't exactly reform him. He just decided it was easier for him to go along with the rules.

Mitchell, in his early days with us . . . I remember at the end of the Infants' portion of Assembly, when it was customary for me to tell the Infants that they might stand, and then that they might leave—Mitchell wouldn't stand. He just sat there; I think as a show of defiance. His teacher June Bowell was a very tall girl, over six feet in height; slender and strong. She had a lovely calm manner with the children. Finally, when she saw what was happening, she simply picked Mitchell up under her arm. His feet were kicking, there, under her arm; but she and the rest of us kept a straight face and said nothing. The children, on the brink of laughter, looked at me—and they all refrained from laughing. And the Infants filed out of the hall in their usual manner.

Now I can remember one other time when a child didn't stand up, when I asked the Infants to stand and leave at the end of their part of assembly. We almost dealt with that too, but fortunately we didn't. He was a little Barnardo's boy, and we found he had muscular dystrophy. He was physically unable to stand without help.

Matthew. I can see him now, sitting, with a look of distress on his face; and the other children standing, looking down at him, puzzled. . . Later, the mothers bought him a tricycle to come to school with. He could get around this way for awhile, if he had someone to help him.

And now I remember still another Barnardo's boy with a physical disability, and he did kick the other boys for awhile, during football. That was Raymond. He was crippled; his periosteum was gone. He wore special boots for his crippled legs and feet, with protective plates for his shins. The other boys in the playground games, just wore soft shoes.

Raymond was passionate for football. The other boys were very good about playing with him, and they were careful of him. But I suppose Raymond got carried away, and he would kick them. Once I was working in my office and there was a tap on my window. It was a group of the boys, with Raymond. One of them said, "Mrs. Ward, would you please have a word with Raymond?" And another, one of the Barnardo's boys, said: "Those bovver boots, don't they 'arf pack a wallop!"

So Raymond was told, and I don't think he kicked any more. He loved football too much.

They were really so good about including someone like that. It must have meant a sacrifice for them: giving up having a first-rate competitive game. One of the boys who lived across the street, his little brother Gary would join them on the lawn, when he was so young—hardly more than a toddler. They would come to me and ask, "Mrs. Ward, may Gary play football with us?" . . . And there they'd be, someone holding Gary's hand, the boys running up and down the field.

But I have wandered. . . . For any other cases of hitting or bullying . . . I have mentioned the case of Anne. . . . There was one of the Barnardo's boys, George, whom I finally had to return to the Doctor Barnardo's Homes, and say we couldn't manage him in our school. I hated to do that. I don't think I ever had to do that with any other child. George was slow in intelligence. He really wasn't so bad, and we would have kept him. However he picked on one of the other boys. We couldn't get him to stop. He couldn't resist. And I felt, strongly, that this other boy should be protected. He seemed to invite bullying. But I was truly sorry that George had to leave the school.

<u>What you can do if you have well-behaved children</u>
What can be done? —I think that is apparent by this time. Lucky teachers!

At Mossford Green: the work of the school could go forward. The children were able to pay attention. They <u>wanted</u> *to do their work. They were interested. They didn't have to be coerced.*

The teacher didn't have to be a disciplinarian. There was no struggle for control of the classroom. She did not even have to raise her voice to be heard. All this extra business of being a teacher—all this diversion—could be dispensed with.

At Mossford Green School: they could do numerous things because of the well-behaved children. These are familiar by now: the flexible scheduling, absence of hall monitors, the classroom routine with pupils working on their own, the crafts groups with their appearance of (organized) chaos, the ritual in Assembly; and more. Teachers didn't have to get the children to line up, form a queue, in order to go somewhere or to wait for something; although the children themselves tended spontaneously to queue up, if they were waiting—for example, to go into the lunchroom or assembly hall.

Outside school, the children's social development can also go forward, in ways which would not be possible otherwise. They can be included in adult activities and groups; they can be allowed to do numerous things, they can be given certain responsibilities—years earlier than otherwise; because they are reliable.

Back to Mossford Green—three more stories:

I can remember, even in university, if my lecture lasted longer than the class period: at once, I would hear a rustling sound. The students were telling me, quite unintentionally,. that they had a right to go—and go at once. Needless to say, it was not this way at Mossford Green. The bell rang; but there was not that stirring and rustling sound. Edna said about this:

. . . When the teacher of the class was satisfied, she would say, "That's all, children. You may stand up." And they would stand in back of their chairs. And she would look about the class to see that everything was all right. Then she would say, "All right. You may put your chairs up." And they put their chairs on top of their desks, in order to help the cleaner. And then: "Good afternoon, children." —"Good afternoon, Mrs. Ward."

Second story:

We had very large windows in the classrooms, which came down low. Allan's dog was an Alsatian—a lovely, lovely dog. He would come for Allan every lunchtime. (Some of the children lived close enough to go home for lunch, and Allan was one of these). Near the time for going home, Allan's mother would let the dog out, and he would go to the school, to the proper window, where Allan was. We could see the tip of his muzzle at the window. He was craning his neck to look in, scanning the room for Allan. . . . and the tip of his tail wagging back and forth.

One of the children would then whisper, "He's come, Mrs. Ward." (Or "he's come," to whomever the teacher was.) Then I'd open the door and in he'd come. Quietly, always. He would come across the room and sit down by Allan's desk. Allan would reach out his hand and pat him. The tail would wag. But that was all. There was no disruption of the class, no playing with him, nothing more in the way of drawing attention to him.

The dog would come at lunch time, to take Allan home for lunch. And he would come again at the end of the day.

We had a child who had very bad asthma. I'll call him Paul. He had to be careful; if he over-exerted or got too excited, he would start gasping. One day I saw Paul coming up the path to school, late, hurrying, almost blue from his asthma. I went out to him and I said "Paul! You *know* you don't have to hurry. You *never* have to hurry like that." It was obvious he had been crying. It took awhile to get the story out of him, but what evidently happened was: a boy—a big boy—two big boys?—stopped him on the way to school, and teased and bullied him in some way, and Paul began to wheeze, and I gather then they teased all the more. They must have been boys from outside the school. Our own children would never have done this.

I said, "Well Paul, you know that no one who matters would ever tease you. And when you grow older, very likely the asthma will get better."

But he was inconsolable. He said, choking back the tears, "It was so uncivilized!"

The Barnardo's children

Doctor Barnardo's Homes is a well-known institution in Britain. Originally they took in homeless children and orphans. I suppose it would be called an orphanage. Nowadays, it is more for children who have been removed from unfit homes. They have a good many residential units; but their main, original, cluster of buildings, was near our school. And their own school for these children had been closed.

I wanted to take in some of the children. One reason was: I had long wanted to have some handicapped children in our school. I thought it would be a good experience for our other pupils. And it seemed a good many of the Barnardo's were obviously handicapped.

I discussed this with the staff and they hated the idea. Whereas our children were mainly middle-class, and they were so well-behaved, and we had things running so well—the Barnardo's children might very well overwhelm us completely. Their previous introduction to school had been negative. They were rough, vulgar. A good many, you might call them: children of the streets. They represented every possible kind of bad influence.

The staff had misgivings. But they could see that we had some obligation here. Since the Barnardo's Homes' own school had been closed, other schools had to absorb these children.

Our parents were worse. They were truly alarmed at my proposal. And they strongly resented it. I could certainly understand that. And I knew I was running a risk by going ahead.

We had to have the confidence of our parents. Our system depended on it. They did so much—they felt included; and they really were. So, for me to simply go ahead in the face of their objections, and bring in the Barnardo's children—I could understand some sense of betrayal on their part. On the other hand we had built up some trust. So they might be willing to go along with it for awhile.

So, in spite of the resistance from everybody—the parents and teachers alike—the Barnardo's children came in. There were about twenty of them in that first lot, coming into our school of three-hundred-fifty pupils.

In subsequent years, fewer came in. They entered in dribs and drabs.

For the first few months, when this started, the parents' worst fears were realized. Their children were exposed to a rich store of sexual mis-information, and vulgar language, which the Barnardo's children brought in. Parents would come in and complain. I tried to keep the choicest tidbits of Barnardo's stories, for these visits. After a complaint had been aired, I would ask the parent, "Well have you heard this one?" And, hopefully, the visit would end with laughter. But I understood: their fear for their children, it was a serious matter.

And she told a story.

One of the Barnardo's children, a little girl, perhaps about eight years old, got one of our little boys to leave the school grounds with her and go to the park. This was a great breach of our rules to begin with. But then she led him into the bushes and she disrobed for him. From what we could understand: what happened next was, there was an awkward moment or two of hesitation. Then the little boy turned away; maybe ran away.

Anyway, later . . . . It took us a while to find them. His mother was distraught. She and I talked to the little boy, together. The little girl's behavior was understandable enough; we knew a bit about her already. But the little boy—I couldn't understand how he could have gone off with her, broken the rules, left the school grounds. But we couldn't get much out of him. He was embarrassed. I asked him, "But why did you *go*?" He finally said, very sheepishly: "I didn't like the view." That broke the tension between the irate mother and myself. We both were laughing.

. . . .

In the classrooms, the new children were of course very disruptive. The teachers did have a lot of trouble at first.

What you all had done in the past, which depended on having very well-behaved children—for example your finger game; and the routine of the classroom, with pupils working on their workbooks and working on group projects; and children going about in the halls without supervision—I guess you couldn't do that, once they were in the school.

No, we tried not to give up any of these things. We tried to keep going just the same. It was hard at first . . . . Then gradually, gradually, it began to get better. The Barnardo's children became not quite so bad. Their academic deficiencies became . . . . not so limiting. They became a bit more able to pay attention and attend to their work. Some friendships were formed between them and our regular pupils. As I said: I think what happened was, in the end, the *ethos* of the school was strong enough to withstand their impact.

As a result of the new friendships, they were invited home to play. . . . invited home to tea . . . .

Some of our parents became fond of particular Barnardo's children. Eventually it reached the point where our parents were paying for them, so they could be included on our end-of-school trips to Europe. (Otherwise, they would not have had the money to go.)

. . . .

What can I say about them, what they were like? It was, in a way, as if a polite, middle-class society had been invaded by street children. With each other, especially, they had a short fuse. They flared up in arguments; they were touchy. I think a key to their behavior was . . . . They hungered for individual attention—someone paying attention, just to them. On the playground, as I've said, it was customary for the adult who was in charge to be holding some child's hand. —The Barnardo's children were competitive, pushy, to get this attention, to be held by the hand.

They would steal things—because they wanted something that belonged to you—perhaps a pocket hankie. And as I say they always wanted to walk round, holding your hand. Claiming you, all the time, trying to mean something to somebody. They were that way with the adults in the school; and with each other. They were desperate for somebody special.

(She told a story.)

Marine, a little black girl, had been told by the authorities, that she was to go live with foster parents. On the appointed day she waited expectantly at the window. She was all dressed up . . . in her ribbons . . . But the foster parents never came for her. They didn't even telephone. I suppose they had changed their minds. One more let-down. Oh dear, you never knew what these children had been deprived of.

On the day when the children took their eleven-plus examinations, each child had a place-card, which had a space for their first name and a space for their second name. Marine came to me and said: "I know I have a second name, and I think it begins with a G. But I never learned what it was."

Marine had said: "When I grow up I shall have a baby and I will never leave it. Never never never." And she did. She brought the baby back to show me. It was a gorgeous little boy. As far as I know, Marine never had anything more to do with the father.

One of the naughtiest children we ever had was another black child, Josie. . . . She had done something to another child . . . And she shouted at me, words to the effect: "Yes and I expect so-and-so's mother will be up to complain about me. But there won't be anyone come up for me." —Always conscious of being alone.

Later, she had to have open heart surgery. She would only go, she said, if Cyril (my husband) and I would go with her and pretend we were her mum and dad. —Difficult, since she was so black.

(Cyril and Edna made a practice of taking children to the doctor. She remembered one case: a child who needed to be taken to the dentist, countless times, for an elaborate series of procedures. The mother couldn't face it. So Edna did it, after school. "It was a special time for the two of us.")

And, with the Barnardo's children, I did get my handicapped children in the school—and with a vengeance. There were some terrible disabilities, among them. A number of them were dying.

We had a spina-bifidum child, Graham, who was brain-damaged; who had no control, so that he dribbled. I can remember Josie exclaiming, "Oh crumbs he burst his bloody bag again! Sir, may I go home for another bag?"

My hope was that my children would learn from association with handicapped children.

Learn? You mean develop empathy with disabled persons? And be caring, help them?

. . . . . Yes. Help them through the day. The Barnardo's children themselves—it was touching—they were *so* protective of each other. So protective of any one of them who was like this. They certainly set a wonderful example in this respect. And our regular children joined in too.

Michael, whose kidneys were failing, was supposed to drink a lot. The children would sit beside him during lunch time, and during snacks, and they'd try to persuade him—"Come on, Michael, just another sip . . . "

Raymond (in his bovver boots, what don't 'arf pack a wallop) was another Barnardo's child, whom they were protective of, and whom they made special allowances for.

Louise, who was pushed about in a wheelchair, who always was bluish in complexion . . . . Then she had heart surgery that was successful. The children noticed: "Oh look she's gone pink!"

Those children seemed to have an awareness of the transience of life. They knew who was going to die and they would talk about it. This was one more contribution, I think, that the Barnardo's children made to our school.

Louise said: "I'm not going to live a very long time, so I better hurry up and learn to read." And again she said, "Pusses don't live for very long, do they?"

And a child said to me, concerned: "Louise says she's not going to live very long. That's not right, is it?" So we talked about that.

Chapter 5

MORAL DEVELOPMENT IN SCHOOL

What did we do in Assembly? —Children put on special programs sometimes. I think I've mentioned some of these, on a theme or topic which a class had been studying. —With dancing or music or a little skit perhaps, in costume. Then there were the Jewish programs which were similar. The local rabbi would organize our Jewish pupils to do these; and they might be in traditional costume. These were to educate the rest of us, to their observances and . . . to their religion. The overall theme, I suppose, was: there are these different religions. But they're all about living together properly. And we know each other.

But, most days, I told a story. We had a prayer, then a hymn, then a story. We were expected to do something religious in Assembly—so, we did this. The stories were sometimes from the Bible; sometimes lives of the saints; and sometimes not necessarily religious. Animal stories: I did a lot of those. I liked Beatrix Potter stories for the very young children. And fables like the tortoise and the hare.

I would read them a story sometimes, instead of telling the story. I remember a book on a Chinese peasant family. I read from that for awhile. Any continuing story like this—I didn't want it to go on for too long. A week was long enough. I didn't want the little ones to lose interest.

Sometimes a child would share the reading with me. This was a particular honor for some pupil who had done something really special. —Such as, for example, writing a really noteworthy paper. I'd congratulate him; and then I'd say, Why don't you help me in Assembly next week? So we would rehearse the story together. I might say: You be Robert in the story. So at those times in the story where Robert would speak, I'd point to it on the page, and he'd read it to the Assembly.

Nearly always the story had a moral—some kind of lesson, some point to it. That is so often the case anyway, with children's stories. If I were telling the story to the Infants as well as to the Juniors—and especially if the Infants were in on the discussion afterwards—the message was something in the nature of . . . doing good. Doing the right thing. Being honest. And doing for others, being kind and considerate—as with the story of Androcles and the Lion. And the Golden Rule. . . .

After the story, we discussed it. If the Infants were included in the discussion, it was on a very childish level as you can imagine. —But sometimes we could go beyond the childish moral of the story. I might ask: How would *you* feel, if someone had done that to *you*? Or: How would *you* feel if you had been put in that situation, or if you had to do that, or if you had to decide about that? And, leading the discussion in this direction, stretched their imaginations—perhaps toward putting themselves in others' shoes. That was my hope at least.

Some of the stories had more to them in the way of problems of moral choice. —Questions like: what might have happened in the story, if the character had done some particular other thing instead? And: What *should* he have done? And: Why should he have done that?

With stories which permitted this kind of discussion, I would let the Infants leave, and then do the discussion with the Juniors, only. Sometimes I waited and discussed it with the older children later in the day; or even on the following day—whenever I happened to be with them.

We encouraged the children to discuss it among themselves, and to think about it—what should have been done, and why. If I had a little time soon afterwards—maybe just five or ten minutes—perhaps with an entire class, or maybe with just a single child, or several of them, I might ask: "What did you think about . . . " (the story). Sometimes—say, when I was walking on the playground—I might hear a snatch of conversation between them. —Earnest discussion, maybe between two little children, sitting on the schoolground.

I would tell them: "If you are talking about something with your friends, and you're not sure what an adult's opinion might be, well come and ask us." And occasionally they did. "Do *you* think that's the proper thing to do?" And on occasion, we got some surprises.

Two little boys came to my office once. "May we speak to you in private, Mrs. Ward?" . . . "With the door shut please?" . . . "I've asked my mum where babies come from, Mrs. Ward, and she'll never tell me. Would you tell me?"

So I did, in a simple way. . . . . If they had been a bit older than that, they would have been far too shy for questions like this. Especially after the Barnardo's children came, with all their lurid talk, their misinformation, there must have been a lot of playground talk along these lines.

Other opportunities for discussions came up, too, that didn't have anything to do with stories I told in Assembly. Wrongdoing by a pupil: that was something which might be discussed.

When a child had committed some transgression, I would talk to him about it. Sometimes this also led to a group discussion. —But not all the time. Sometimes the child would be too embarrassed so we'd keep it private. Anyway, I would speak to him in my office, and I'd try to draw it out of him—why it was wrong, what he had done; what the principle was. If it was a rule which he had broken: why there had to be that rule. As in the group discussions: I never wanted to *tell* them. I always tried to get *them* to tell *me*. Of course I gave them a little help—as little help as possible.

As a discussion leader, Edna had considerable power to direct the discussion and shape the answers, by the questions she asked. I believe she was an artful discussion leader, with a light touch, not heavy-handed. I think she did manage to avoid telling them. Instead, the children themselves enunciated the principles, came up with the "answers".[1]

After we had gone on like this for awhile—if I thought the child was up to it—I'd say: Look, you know what the answer is here, you understand this. Can we discuss this in class? And ninety percent of the time, the child would say yes.

Can you tell me a few of these?

Yes. . . . Yes. There were some gorgeous ones.

Simon Cramp—he was so brilliant—committed a transgression once, I remember. Children had their musical instruments, and other persons weren't supposed to touch them. —Only the child who owned the instrument could. And Simon, once, did fiddle with a clarinet which didn't belong to him; and it must have fallen out of his hands; because he broke something. —And I think he must have been horrified. But he did later confess.

So Simon and I, we went through this process together. First we talked in my office. He could see right away: the principle, why there was this particular rule. —"Don't handle other people's musical instruments." —Because you could damage them. He didn't have to be brilliant to see that.

In the group discussion which we finally had, Simon said something else. He said that everyone should have an experience like this—committing a crime and getting caught. It gave you more compassion for people who get caught, who are disgraced. You are not so quick to condemn.

<u>When the football team went on a shoplifting spree</u>

The boys had gone to another playing field for a game after school. But it rained, hard, and the game was called off. The coach bade them good evening and went home. There they were, feeling very let down.

They stopped into a Woolworths, maybe to get out of the rain, and they were aimlessly wandering around. One boy said something like: "I'll bet I can pick up this package of hairpins and put it in my pocket and the shop girl won't even notice." Maybe another boy said he couldn't. So he did. It was easy. I imagine they were surprised. So another boy tried it. He too had no trouble. So, I daresay: a kind of reckless mood seized them.

They stole the most ridiculous things. Not candies or anything that a boy might want; but . . . one boy picked up a roll of cotton cloth. And there were other items of this nature. Hairspray, Kirbi grips which women put in their hair. Needles and pins—sewing equipment. Finally the inevitable happened. They were caught in the act.

Later the Woolworths manager came to see me at the school. He was a lovely man; I had known him already. He said that the shop did have a problem with that sort of thing. He couldn't simply let it go and forgive it.

I sent for the boys. And I confronted them with the Woolworths manager. And I sent for their mothers. I put the boys in one of the classrooms, and they waited for their mums to arrive at the school. You can imagine: there were a few tears shed. Anyway, as we waited, and as the parents began to arrive, this turned into a discussion of sorts.

The boys said they certainly didn't go into the shop with the idea of stealing. Somehow—one thing led to the next—it just happened that way. I think they themselves couldn't understand how it happened. It was such a lapse. It was so uncharacteristic of them. Their parents were mortified of course. And this deepened their shame even more.

The moral of this story—what I wanted them to say for themselves—was: you have to be trustworthy. When your teacher goes home, when nobody is watching, you *still* have to be trustworthy. Otherwise: and they knew what the "otherwise" was, they could feel it—their shame.

Anyway, the way it all turned out was: I had them bring the stolen items to me. Then I had one of the boys write a letter of apology to the Woolworths' manager. Then, on a later day, we all trooped down to the Woolworths—the boys, with a few of their parents, and myself. We formed a crocodile *(a line, two-abreast)* and went down the sidewalk. Ceremonially, in this fashion, we entered the shop; we returned the items to the manager; and the boy read his letter.

The manager was extremely gracious; he had been, throughout. Later he brought back a huge box of chocolates for the boys. Of course we couldn't have that—a reward. So the teachers themselves ate the chocolates in the staff lounge.

<u>The maturing of a moral sense</u>

Edna used such opportunities as came to her, for moral training. Some of these were fairly standard for British schools. This is true for stories in Assembly, with discussion. It is also true for charity appeals. Other schools do this too. Mossford Green, perhaps, did it with a bit extra. In addition, a sense of school pride and school honor was encouraged, and the giving of gifts.

I once listened to her, talking to another veteran teacher about children's moral development in school. It was interesting to hear their notions about how children change as they get older. At first the little children could only follow rules, such as, "When the bell rings, get ready to come in off the playground." And they were egoistic. Then they changed, and other kinds of moral thinking were possible. The change was not gradual; it was stepwise. All at once, Edna would notice for the first time: a little boy had made a statement of right-and-wrong; and it was a statement of principle, not necessarily centered in himself. He was thinking in a different fashion; the <u>way</u> he thought had changed.

What these teachers recognized—this step-wise progress—bore some resemblance to the psychological theories of cognitive-moral development;[2] but not too much, really. The teachers' thinking was less formalized of course; and they recognized fewer stages. Edna was aware of two step-up points when children's thinking obviously changed: at about age seven; and again at about age ten. Actually the age-points were not clear-cut: seven or somewhat sooner; nine or ten-ish. Bright children could make the step much sooner. Slow children were slower and might never see the light; at least not while they were in her school.

The first step-up involved being able to see general principles of fairness and justice and consideration, as applying to other persons, not solely to one's self. "That wasn't fair to <u>me</u>!"—moral indignation—can extend to "That wasn't fair!" (to him). "Mrs. Ward, Anne took Jeremy's lunch!"

"Mrs. Ward—Raymond is pushing the Infants out of their place in the queue! He's getting in ahead of them!" Edna mentions this as an instance where a child makes the step and she notices it for the first time: not "he's pushing me out of my place in the queue," but instead

"he's pushing the Infants" —he's pushing others. Or: it's not right to push in, even if I myself am not involved. The child is tattling on Raymond too; but that is something else. They were encouraged to do this.

If children, when they achieve this stage, are capable of getting exercised over principles of fairness and the like, then: what effect do the stories have, with the stories' moral "lessons;" and the discussion afterwards? —Presumably, the children are now "old enough." "He shouldn't have done that"—in the story—"because it wasn't fair" is now meaningful to them. A more differentiated awareness of general principles; and being able to see them as applying to situations—this can now be helped along, by the stories, and the discussion. —For those children who have matured to the point where they are ready to think in this fashion. This is the hope at least.[3]

Edna recognized another kind of moral development at an early age. This was by way of "How would you feel if . . ." The child's capacity for empathy, putting himself in another's shoes and feeling with another—which is ordinarily present in a primitive form, from about age two[4] —this can be appealed to. Even before abstract moral concepts can be comprehended, some progress can be made.

You don't say to a little child: "It's wrong to . . ." (whatever). Instead you might say "How would *you* feel if (someone) took your (whatever)?" At first, even words like to lie, to steal, are too abstract. Instead you must say "took your . . ." At first, even honesty, truthfulness, is an abstraction which the child is not ready for.

When little children (pre-school) are cruel, and hit and pinch, you can say, "Look, if I were to bite you, would you like it?" . . . They are very caught up in themselves. So you can relate back to that too.

It is very odd, building up a sense of . . . all the values we take for granted . . . from this beginning point.

. . . It is a big step, getting children out of themselves and able to think in terms of principles, and able to apply these to situations.

Whereas, in the beginning, moral indignation is in defense of Me—"That wasn't fair to Me!" "He took My things!"

Edna felt that the change in the children's thinking style, at around age seven, was not entirely to the good. Awareness of Principle came in. However some of the delightful childish qualities receded. The children's artwork lost some of its charm and originality. It became more mannered, more "realistic." —All-of-a-piece, presumably, with the overall cognitive reorganization which was taking place.

The second step up, at about age ten, was less clear to me. Possibly it was less clear and definite to Edna too, as a discreet stage. She only knew: her older children, her Juniors, began to be more grown-up in their discussions. They would debate what a character in a story should have done, and why; and what the consequences might have been if he had done something else. "They could go on by the hour if I let them:" stating the application of principles to situations; arguing points, making distinctions. They relished it.

Also, the brighter pupils were capable of originality and insight. —As with Simon Cramp when he damaged the clarinet: "Everyone has to make some mistakes in life now and then. When you do, (and when you are shamed like he had been), then you can become more understanding of other people. You can sympathise with them when they do wrong things."

<u>What moral principles?</u>

Here are a few:

The lessons to the stories were in the nature of Honesty is the Best Policy; lying and cheating get you into trouble; be kind and generous and you will be rewarded.

There was group of good-citizen principles: follow the rules, be honorable and trustworthy, do your duty. Fairness was important.

The teachers tried to promote a good-citizenship code for the school, which included the rule, <u>don't retaliate.</u> Here, Edna had a story:

A little boy was brought to her with small wooden blocks stuffed into his ear. They were wedged in tight; they wouldn't come out. What had happened was this: His classroom had been working on their maths, *in which these blocks were used in the calculations, somewhat like Cuisinaire blocks. He was working along, and he found to his irritation: when he needed to use a block he couldn't find one, because the little girl next to him had taken them. "Mrs. Ward, Angela kept taking my blocks!" Angry, but mindful of the injunction not to retaliate—at a loss as to what to do, he continued, preoccupied with his maths problems. And he put the blocks for safe keeping into his ear. He hadn't wanted to make any fuss. But now, in the end, there <u>was</u> all this fuss. Edna went with him to the Surgery, and the little blocks were removed.*

In the more mature discussion by the Juniors, the consequences of actions and decisions came to the fore. And some of the complications could be brought out. Thinking of the effect on other persons—what would result if you did this or that—could get very complicated.

Also, more than one principle might come to bear on a decision; and these could conflict. There was much to argue about and debate. "They began to see some of the dilemmas."

(In Edna's own life, I know, honoring prior commitments, keeping promises, is an over-riding principle. It leads her into doing things which she otherwise wouldn't do, which she sometimes hates doing, which she might even think are wrong.)

<u>Acting on principle</u>

A source of amusement was the Infants' mastery of safety rules for crossing the street. In safety drill they might do it perfectly and never forget. But out on the street, they tended to forget the rules and cross willynilly. They hadn't yet gotten to the point of acting on the rules in real life. The older Juniors laughed, and helped to keep an eye on them.

There is a big difference of course, between seeing the application of a principle or a rule, and actually acting on it. For the children, even if they "remembered," still, acting in accordance with a moral principle might go against what they had wanted to do. Edna's hope was that they would, eventually, become this way—"not just doing things to please themselves, or to get praise for doing it"—but even if they wouldn't be seen doing the virtuous act, even if they would not be praised, doing it anyway.

<u>Consideration</u>

Another guiding principle, or group of principles, is considera-tion—being aware of other people's needs, and acting accordingly. Perhaps the Golden Rule—"do unto others . . . "—covers this. However I prefer to think of consideration as an outgrowth of empathy and sympathy—that (originally) primitive childish trait.

The evolution of childish empathy into grown-up consideration can be viewed as a line of moral development all on its own. Discussions such as Edna conducted, in which the "how would <u>you</u> feel if . . . " question is asked, can further it along. With increasing maturity, consideration becomes more and more refined. And, by way of the "how would <u>you</u> feel" question, different kinds of consideration emerge: not only kindness and generosity and thoughtfulness, but also patience with other people, and tact, and respect for their privacy, and tolerance (as with Simon Cramp's example).

Edna thought that this process was well on its way by the time her Juniors left Mossford Green, at about age eleven. Consideration would go on becoming more refined, as they got older still. But they had made the basic transition: "to looking out from within themselves, to other people, and recognizing that others have needs too."

She said:

One of our discussions must have touched on children with handicaps. A Barnardo's child said, "Everybody's got handicaps. But some handicaps show, and some do not." This seemed to have struck a chord. There was a murmur of response to this, throughout the group.

After school one day, a piece of paper was left lying on the schoolground. We found out later: it was an Infant's artwork for the day. He had dropped it as he'd left school. He must have been taking it home to show his mum. That's what the Infants did every day.

Anyway, other children were playing on the schoolground after school. And one of them snatched it up, in the course of his play with the others, and he hastily crumpled it into a ball and tossed it at another child.

Of course he had no idea it belonged to anybody any more; or that it was valued by anybody. But as it turned out, it was. The Infant finally realized he'd dropped his paper. And he went back and looked for it; and other children helped him search; and they finally found what was left of it, wet and torn, crumpled of course.

The child was inconsolable. And, at some point, I was told of this catastrophe.

I don't remember too much about the ensuing discussion—what form it took. Anyway, the point of it was—what I wanted them to see was—the Infant was taking his paper home to his mum. I wanted them to remember how important that was, at that age. —And to imagine, how crestfallen the child must have been. And, to my mind at least, the point was: you cannot be heedless, as in that kind of heedless play, throwing the crumpled paper. It's all right to play, but you have to be mindful of others. —Of the consequences of what you do, for others. In the case of this older boy: maybe he hadn't even done anything wrong. But the consequences of what he did were dramatic. I think he felt sorry about it. So I suppose that was part of the lesson too: it's hard not to make a mistake sometimes. —A rather grown-up lesson, really.

<u>Cards, gifts, and charities</u>

—All these were part of the same training—to get the children to look outside themselves. It started with the Infants, making cards to take home to their mums. And making cards for other people, for their teachers. Writing little letters. Making little pots from clay, in crafts.

Then as they get older, age six, age seven, they are capable of being conscious of other people outside their immediate circle of home and school. Then, when they can be aware of other children elsewhere, you can introduce them to simple charities, simple things they can do.

British schools across the nation raise funds for charities. We at Mossford Green might have a number of drives and appeals going on at the same time; and we were not unusual in this respect. The children raised the money in different ways. One popular method was by . . . . I think you in America would call it "—athon." Walkathon or whatever.

Here we would call it a sponsored walk. Or a sponsored spelling bee. Or . . . you know.

News of disasters, famines, earthquakes, especially those which might affect children—we brought this to the school's attention. —Not in any horrific way. But we did talk about it. And we might put a poster up. We probably gave more emphasis to appeals for other British children, in other parts of Britain. —Anything to make it easier for them to identify with these others.

A good example of a nationwide appeal was the Aberfan disaster in Wales. There was a mud slide from a mining tip. It covered up much of the Aberfan school. Other schools across Britain helped them rebuild. We bought a new piano for them.

In these cases, we asked the children: how should we raise the money? They enjoyed coming up with . . . all sorts of gorgeous ideas. A sponsored silence. —How many minutes they could keep silent, sitting at lunch hour. Another: a sponsored hymn sing after Assembly. A child earned five *p* for the appeal, with every hymn she sang. Of course the parents were the main donors. The money for all these appeals must have come mainly from the parents. But I gave, too. For the hymn sing, after every hymn I would scrabble in my handbag for the five *p*. Another: a sponsored swim, held in the swimming baths; a child earned for the appeal, by how many lengths she could swim. Parents came to these too. The mood could become hilarious. Another: a sponsored read-in; so much money for every page a child could read in . . . so many minutes. For the older children, we had a sponsored book-read, so much for every book. I would check them by asking them a question about their book.

For the Ethiopian famine, they knitted little squares. Then we stitched these together into blankets.

All this was outside of class-time. I would get up a note to the parents, make sure it wasn't too inconvenient, invite them to come.

Safety Sam's retirement
The children sent cards and gifts too. When our French caretaker retired, they all wrote something nice about him, and thanked him for his care for the school. This was all put into a folio, along with artwork they

had made. And it was given to him—a farewell present from the children.

This was a sort of standard thing when someone retired. I myself have a huge folio from the children, fifteen inches square, decorated with lacey artwork on the cover. This was for when I myself retired.

With such a farewell gift, all the children would take part. Their names would be on it, and any other contributions of artwork or writing. —Each person, trying to say meaningful things, recalling perhaps something memorable about the person which had happened. —And making compliments, appropriate compliments.

I think you can see how this looks forward to being thoughtful in adulthood, in the manner of remembering to send a card or a gift, and saying kind things.

When Safety Sam retired—he had throat cancer—we held long discussions about what to give him. The children finally decided on a nice comfortable easy chair to sit in, after his years of service, standing at the street crossing. The children discussed: Who would make the presentation? Safety Sam—When a child didn't obey his crossing-instructions, and simply ran heedlessly across the street, then Safety Sam would "arrest" him. He would take the child into custody, and march him into my office. So, they said, Christopher had been arrested so many times—he should present the chair.

On Safety Sam's day, we held the ceremony in the Assembly hall. We sat him in the front, in his chair, and we sang his favorite song for him. It was really very emotional, as these group-recognitions tend to be. I myself had to fight back the tears.

. . . . . . You can see where we're going with all this. Some of these events might have happened anyway, even if we weren't always looking for a chance to . . . to get the children to thinking along these lines. —To extend their thinking in this way.

With present-giving, you try to put yourself in the other person's place. You use your imagination: what would he want? What would be the spot-on best thing to give? . . . . . And then you do it. Then, hopefully, the children feel good about it.

This is significant in that: just so many opportunities were offered to Edna, to give moral-training experiences. The stories and discussions gave no chance for the children to <u>do</u> anything. And real-life morality requires action, doing it, often at personal cost and inconvenience. This present-giving gave a small opportunity for that.

To review briefly: there were the stories with discussions; and discussions following children's misdemeanors; and fund-raisers for charities, which were preceded by news of far-away persons who were in need; and the giving of cards and presents; and retirement-days. Also there was the normal everyday life of the school, which might have been more important as moral training than any of these.

The various moral principles which have been mentioned, I would group into two types:

One type is consideration in all its forms, developing out of early childish empathy, by way of "how would <u>you</u> feel if . . . " —Putting yourself in another's place, and then being able to act on this.

"An Englishman's Word Is His Bond"

The other type is principles such as Be Honest, Keep Your Promises, Honor Your Obligations, and the good-citizenship code for the school, which included such rules as Don't Retaliate, and Don't Take Advantage (in such situations as a queue).

These are very important. For example honesty and keeping promises is the basis for trust. Trust in a community is a precious thing to have. (You will have noted how the children were trusted: with money, in the halls, marking their own papers.)

How does a person come to be trustworthy, honest? —There are probably multiple reasons. One possible reason is: He sees himself as an honorable person. This is important to him. This self-image would be threatened if he made a slip . So this keeps the person more or less in line.

And how does it come about that it's important to a person, to see himself as a man of honor? —One possible source of this is: he belongs to a regiment, or to an aristocratic family, or to an officers' corps, or to some other group, which has a code of honor. He is proud to belong. It is important to him. And to make a slip would be to let them down.

In <u>The English Gentleman</u>, Philip Mason recounts the changing codes of honor throughout the centuries. These included the gambler's code, the country gentleman's code during the 19th century, and an earlier code of <u>gentillesse</u> which applied to women too. Honesty was not all that was required. But honesty was part of what was involved in being honorable.[5]

British schools, with their school uniforms, school songs, and competition with other schools, do seem to have some pride-in-belonging. Edna felt the Infants were thrilled to wear the uniform for the first time; and to make the big step up, to going to school. She tried to capitalize on this.

At Mossford Green, there seemed to have been a sense of school honor. I asked her how she tried to encourage this.

You want to make the children feel that they are valued; they're valued members of their community, that is to say, of the school. You give them responsibilities. They make their contributions. Then you give them recognition.

The recognition would not come in the form of prizes and awards; but rather it would come as mention during Assembly, and thanks. Each child felt that Edna knew him personally; the two of them went over his papers together.

Then there is the school uniform and the singing and all the special times together as well.

So sense of belonging, of one-ness, builds up; and school pride is somehow connected with that. A child doesn't want to let the others down. To disgrace the school, would be terribly shameful. And the football players did disgrace the school. They dishonored it before the public, before Woolworths. I hope it made a lasting impression on them.

So school honor helped maintain a high standard at Mossford Green. Did some of this stay with the children after they left? —We don't know. Hopefully so.

Credit should be given to the parents too, for the foundation they provided. We've mentioned before, how the children were susceptible to appeals to conscience. A teacher could talk to them, "and make them to understand that they had done something wrong." As Edna said when I inquired about any scolding:

"Scolding? What was the point of scolding?" (*As with the football boys when they had been brought to her, after shoplifting:*) "They all stood before me with their heads hanging down . . . some in tears . . . ."

The occasional child such as Matt, who was not vulnerable in this way, had a sort of inner freedom which the other children lacked. He could defy the adults and go on his way. The difference was so marked—it made all the more clear, the susceptibility of the other children. The children's conscience gave an enormous advantage to the teachers.

Edna told one more story about the weight of public shaming. This was another story of shoplifting at Woolworths.

Hillary had a crush on Eric Nichols. When Eric's birthday came: she went to Woolworth's and, in her impulsive way, stole a man's shirt, wrapped in cellophane. She later presented it to him. Eric was embarrassed by this surprise gift of the too-large shirt. He took it home and showed it to his mother, who brought it in to Edna, and together they guessed what must have happened. They confronted Hillary.

Edna told her she would have to take it back and apologize. Hillary begged Edna to go along with her. So, once more, they went to Woolworths. When they came face-to-face with the shop's manager, Hillary was tongue-tied. The man was graciousness itself—as always. So Edna had to make the apology speech on Hillary's behalf.

What makes a child susceptible? And another child like Matt, not? —We won't add to the volumes of psychology on conscience-development, beyond these two points:

Edna thinks, for the school as a whole, it is important that pupils respect the staff; this makes appeals to conscience more effective.

These searing incidents of shaming: how much lasting power do they have? —I think, in my own case, one of these events was good for a lifetime. But of course we don't know about other cases. What kind of behavior gets shamed: this probably has much to do with whether the lesson is lasting or not.

Charlie Schmidt was teaching me hunting. We two little boys were walking down the railroad track with Charlie's BB gun; and we had taken a couple of shots at birds; when a housewife walked across to us and began to scold us for what we were doing. Charlie walked ahead out of range of the scolding. I stopped and took it; then went on; but I think this was the end of my hunting career.

<u>Notes</u>
1.   Research up to now indicates that discussion is more effective than preaching, for moral education. This is summarized in

Sheldon Berman. *Children's Social Consciousness and the Development of Social Responsibility*. Albany, NY: SUNY Press, 1997: 111.

2.   Berman, pp. 50ff, 79-80, 94ff.

William Kurtines and Jacob Gewirtz (eds.) *Moral Development: An Introduction*. New York: Allyn and Bacon, 1995: 17-134.

Barry Chazam. *Contemporary Approaches To Moral Education: Analyzing Alternative Theories*. New York: Teachers College Press, 1985.

Nel Noddings. *Philosophy of Education*. Dimensions of Philosophy Series. Boulder, Colo.: Westview Press, 1995: 70-77, 153.

Lawrence Kohlberg. *The Philosophy of Moral Development: Moral Stages and the Idea of Justice*. San Francisco: Harper and Row, 1981.

Kohlberg. *The Psychology of Moral Development*. San Francisco: Harper and Row, 1984.

Joseph Reimer, Diana Paolitto, and Richard Hersh. *Promoting Moral Growth*. New York: Longman, 1983.

3. Researchers disagree on the age at which a child can recognize transgressions—possibly as early as age two—and have some comprehension of general rules of behavior..

Berman (*op. cit.*) p. 23.

Martin Hoffman, "The contribution of empathy to justice and moral judgement." In Bill Puka, ed. *Moral Development*, volume one. New York: Garland, 1994: 161-165.

Reimer, Paolitto, and Hersh (*op. cit.*) 1983: 48.

4. Martin Hoffman, "Empathy, its development and prosocial implications." In C. B. Keasey, ed. *Nebraska Symposium On Motivation*. Volume 25, pp. 169-227. Lincoln: University of Nebraska Press, 1978.

Hoffman 1994 (*op. cit.)* 1994: 165, 167, 172, 174, 178, 183.

Kohlberg (*op. cit.*), 1984: 71, 74-75, 171.

Nancy Eisenberg, *Altruistic Emotion, Cognition, and Behavior*. Hillsdale, NJ: Lawrence Erlbaum, 1986: 30-56.

John C. Gibbs, "The cognitive development perspective." In Kurtines and Gerwirtz,, (*op. cit.*) 1995: 42-43.

5.   Philip Mason. *The English Gentleman: the Rise and Fall of an Ideal*. London: Pimlico, 1982.

Chapter 6

COMMENTS BY FORMER PUPILS, TEACHERS, AND PARENTS AT MOSSFORD GREEN

I interviewed twenty-two persons in addition to Edna herself: former pupils and their parents, and seven former teachers—June Bowell, Malcolm Griffin, Brenda Lambert, Joan Lumley, Lilian Opposs, Beryl Parr, and Leslie Steinman.

There were some disagreements. For one thing there were changes over time. My questioning of Edna had glossed over these. Also, in her position as Head, she simply hadn't known about some of the bad things that had occurred. Several of the (then) boys now admitted to school pranks that she had never known about.

There were disagreements about the size of the classes. Edna had spoken of classes with thirty children in them. This seemed so large. How could the hard-pressed teachers give the necessary personal attention? But it turned out that sometimes the classrooms had up to thirty-nine children in them. Four of the teachers remembered classes that were this large.

So how had the teachers managed? Edna had said that parents helped in the classroom. But for much of the time, especially in the early years, this was not the case. How, then, had they managed?

Student-teachers were sent to the school; and they had served as teachers' helpers in a few of the classes. In addition, Joan Lumley said that she herself had her more advanced pupils helping the less advanced ones. But mostly the teachers—as one said—"simply worked very hard."

Still, the different ability-groups were a problem: how to serve them all? Joan Lumley said that she racked her brain, trying to give the brighter pupils challenging things to do. She worried that she hadn't enough time to give all the individual attention that was needed.

Reading through Edna's account, there are many points at which somebody differs with her. How an Infant first came to school with his mother; the ceremony of signing the Register in which the Infant receives his pencil and gets a lesson in handwriting from Edna; later, the Teddies sitting in their little chairs; still later, what went on in school Assembly . . . (One boy remembered that it was his birthday, three separate times in about a half-year, hoping to get the birthday sweets.) . . . Sports Days . . . the school pets . . . . (One teacher didn't remember that the Infants were ever invited to help feed the pets); the children's work at school. Assessment sheets . . . Trouble with the Barnardo's children: several persons spoke of this, but one former pupil remembered no trouble at all, only Barnardo's friends. Handicapped children in the school: one teacher remembered very few. And so the comments went.

Several persons spoke about the children's competitiveness. It sounded as if the school was less successful than Edna had remembered, in downplaying this. Malcolm Griffin told a story about Sports Day. The children who ran in the races were given their little prizes, irrespective of how they had finished. But then one child had asked, "Yes, but who won?" Malcolm said: "This was a shock to us." (-to the staff) He talked of the "outside world breaking in on us." Evidently they were hoping to create a little noncompetitive milieu within the school, in which the competitiveness of the outside world had been replaced by kindlier sentiments. —And yet here it was, coming in from somewhere, breaking into their school activities.

There was considerable disagreement with Edna when it came to the topic of school discipline and children's misbehavior. Eleven persons saw more misbehavior than Edna had remembered. There were a few extra bullies whom Edna hadn't known about. More fights were mentioned too. And two boys described pranks of the mischief-makers.

Here is one of the stories of bullying:

One mother's little daughter, who was "shy and quiet," was being "blackmailed" by another girl at school. This went on for some time, threats of the nature of "I'll get the other girls never to talk to you, unless you . . ." (do what she wanted her to do). Edna, when questioned, finally began to remember about this blackmailing little girl. The girl had been something of an outcast, as Edna remembered. She smelled, and the other children tended to avoid her. What she wanted of this other child, evidently, was that she be her only friend, exclusively, and not even speak to the other children.

The threatening continued. The mother was worried. She urged her daughter to stand up to the bully; but this was asking quite a lot, more than the little girl could do.

Finally, after repeated urgings from her mother, the little girl came home one day, excited, and told how she had finally gotten up her courage and spoken back to this other girl. She had told her:

"My mum told me to tell you to sod off! So bloody well sod off!" She was proud and exhilarated. (This was such an atypical thing for her to say; so unladylike.) " . . . and Mrs. Ward said she was giving me a gold star!" (—for standing up for herself.)

The misbehavior which is reported, is nearly all sub rosa, out of the view of the teachers. Challenging authority was extremely rare. However, it did happen—rarely, but it was not completely unknown. For example, one teacher remembered a boy who was ejected from class and sent to the office, who never went to the office. He simply left the school building and went home instead. And we have this story from another boy:

Edna, when telling about lunch period, had described how pairs of older children played the part of mother and father at the lunchroom table. They served the Infants at their table from serving bowls; then they asked if anybody wanted seconds; and they urged any reluctant little diner to at least try a little bit. Then they carried all the bowls and plates back to the kitchen at the end of the meal. However, this is what the boy said that he and his friends had done. They were impatient to finish lunch, finish their duties, go outside and play football during the rest of the lunch period. So they rushed their Infants through their meal. As he remembers it, this was so blatant that it was finally discovered, and they couldn't play the parent role at the lunchroom table anymore.

But, people said, even though it might not have been as peaceful as Edna had remembered—still, the children were very good. June Bowell's term was "amenable." The children were very amenable. Even the boy, formerly a mischief-maker, described the school as a "happy family." The teacher who had given a detailed commentary with the most disagreements with Edna, still made clear that the school was "very happy and well behaved." Other teachers who had given detailed commentaries, likewise agreed with the overall picture Edna had given, of extremely good behavior. And the other people, too, spoke of how well behaved the children had been.

Malcolm Griffin disagreed on one point. Edna had made it sound as if the children had come from middle-class homes that had trained them to be very well behaved to begin with. The school only had to continue this. He thought this was misleading; the families were "mostly middle-class" in that the people worked in offices. But there weren't too many professional people among them. Lower middle-class, sociologists would call them.

Be that as it may—he said, the potential for naughtiness was in the children; and not merely in the Bernardo's children. The "good" children, too, could have caused trouble. Even Simon Cramp had his moods.

(He spoke of Simon, who had once fastened himself onto a doorway like a spiderweb, so that nobody could leave the classroom. He thought Simon was so imaginative that he was sometimes frustrated by his own ideas. "His imagination went faster than what he could do, so he got very frustrated at times." Malcolm remembered one class assignment: carve something out of a cake of soap. Simon had visualized two ferrets running up a tree. That is what he wanted to make and, naturally, his efforts failed. He couldn't do it, and that angered him.)

There were also those very few children, such as Matt, who wanted to cause trouble. Malcolm Griffin searched his memory and came up with three more like this. They tried to divert attention to themselves, get the other children to laugh at them, disrupt the class. But they had no luck with this. They were merely regarded as pests. An instigator-child might be told by his neighbors in the classroom, "Oh go away."

This was because the children in the class were so interested in what they were doing that they didn't want this kind of interruption. —Several people said this.

Why were they so interested? Numerous reasons were given: Edna's interest in what they were doing, their parents' interest, the artfulness of teachers . . . (Joan Lumley said, "If you can lead them, they'll do anything for you") . . . . the creative nature of some of the class projects . . . (Edna described a spacecraft in Malcolm's classroom made out of old chairs).

One of the mothers said: the children didn't follow the lead of a troublemaker child "because they respected the teachers." Edna said: "These children would never be disrespectful to one of us." (As we've seen, this wouldn't be true for Matt, and probably for a few others.)

Nor were there any acts of disrespect to the school as a whole. In all her years, she couldn't remember a single case of disfiguring school property, writing on the walls, not any kind of vandalism.

When I did the interviews I was asking for disagreements. But the main comments I heard were accolades. The parents expressed their gratitude. One mother spoke of Edna's way with the children; how she knew each child individually; how Edna had coaxed her own shy little daughter into first coming into the school; and what a terrible, tearful time it had been, when Edna had retired. Simon Cramp's mother spoke of how "wonderful" Edna had been with him, and how keenly oriented she had been, to his welfare. There was a "wonderful feeling . . . of care . . . in that school . . . All the staff (knew) all the children." Another mother spoke of Edna's hospitality, how she herself had felt at home in the school; and she described the welcome which Edna extended to all the parents. The parents, and the teachers also, spoke of the spirit and feeling within the school.

Joan Lumley said that the ethos of the school "was lovely, really wonderful . . . a happy school." But she went on to say that "you can't really put it (the feeling) into words." She said about Edna: "Her door was always open." The older children—having graduated from Mossford Green and gone on to secondary school—would sometimes come back and visit. A few of the former pupils might be sitting at the back during an Assembly. Or, when their own school let out a little earlier in the afternoon than did Mossford, they would come back—"to see Mrs. Ward and tell her what they had been doing, and sometimes to ask her for advice."

Joan talked about the swimming baths, the children in the water being taught how to swim. Some of them were afraid at first. She described how gently these children were treated. They were told: "Just watch. You don't have to go in the water." So they watched at first; but then, without pressuring, they would eventually do it.

One boy was slow in his progress, slow to get over his fear; but he was finally able to swim a little bit. —Then it was later undone by his secondary schoolmaster who made the boy jump in at the deep end.

This I think could be taken as a metaphor for Edna's teaching style, slow and gentle, accepting of babyish behavior, coaxing children out of their fearfulness—as contrasted with the manly throw-him-in-the-deep-water approach.

Regarding the spirit and motivation of the teachers themselves, Malcolm Griffin had this to say. —And this helps to explain how they were able to give personal attention, and teach separate ability-groups, in their very large classes. Edna tended to attract to her staff, people who shared her conception of education. There were several who didn't; but most did.

"We felt we were on the cutting edge." He spoke of a spirit of innovation, then, in the teaching field. Not only were they themselves on the cutting edge; "there were others too, in other schools. We were going back and forth, trying to (learn from the experience in each other's schools), and work out the best way of doing these things."

He said that Edna, with her staff, transmitted their enthusiasm to each other. At lunch time, every day, all the teachers ate lunch together in the staff lounge. In this room which was usually occupied by Mrs. Opposs and her Special Help, the group convened. Edna sat at the head of the table. "If some kind of (event or special happening) was coming up, we planned it" (at lunch time). Discussions about teaching and the school were leavened with laughter. Edna had said in another connection that after every school day, she "took home delightful stories about the children." This came into the staff meetings as well.

Malcolm thought the great enthusiasm of the teachers, why they had worked so hard, was renewed in these staff meetings; and in other ways it was encouraged by Edna. But it also was a product of that particular era. (In our modern era, we see the opposite: discouragement of the teachers, transmitted down from above.)

But to sum up, here, what these teachers and parents and former pupils said: They did have some incidental disagreements with Edna's version. There were some changes in the school over time, so that her generalizations about the thirteen-year period should have been qualified. Some of the children's misbehaviors, she had never known about—or perhaps she had forgotten. Having said that, I think her overall version of the school still stands.

Chapter 7

BRITISH SCHOOLS TODAY

Edna retired in 1977. The National Curriculum was voted in, in 1988.[1] People felt that something like this was necessary. Schools needed tightening up. And some comparability would be nice, from one part of the country to the next. Certain things should be taught to all children. —So a National Curriculum was welcomed in.[2]

Perhaps this was not a bad idea. The unintended consequence was—the bureaucratic baggage that came with it. As I've mentioned before: there were many forms and reports for the teachers and Heads to fill out; and inspections to prepare for. And what they taught was forced into a standardized format.[3] When we asked teachers: could Edna have done what she did today, in the era of the National Curriculum? —the answer they gave was generally no.

The weight of this fell less hard on secondary school teachers. In our interviewing, we actually found a few who liked the new regime. Younger teachers, who started work after the National Curriculum had come in, were less dissatisfied than were the older teachers. As for private schools: the few we interviewed in, tended to go along with the new system; so their teachers did not escape it.

Primary schools—such as Mossford Green—took the brunt of it. Older primary school teachers and Heads, who had taught prior to 1988, expressed the most pain. There were early-retirements, en masse. There were "nervous breakdowns," especially among school Heads.[4]

Teachers complained, teachers left. This did not seem to make any difference. Government churned on. No authoritative person seems to have looked at the schools to see what was happening. That this could occur to a great educational tradition—this is a caution to all of us.

What we are left with is the story of Edna's school, Mossford Green. It is a demonstration of what school and education can be.

<u>Notes</u>

1.	Bob Moon. *A Guide to the National Curriculum*. Third edition, Oxford University Press, 1996: p. 1.

2.	Moon 1996: 10-15.

	Michael Barber. *The National Curriculum: A Study In Policy*. Keele University Press, 1996.

	The Times Educational Supplement, December 25, 1998: p. 6.

3.	Barber (*op. cit.*).

	The Times Educational Supplement (*op. cit.*).

4.	Tim Brighouse, "In search of infallibility." *The Times Educational Supplement*, November 27, 1998: 15.

	The Times Educational Supplement (*op. cit.*) p. 1, and December 4, 1998, p. 7.

ACKNOWLEDGMENTS

We did much visiting and conversing with other persons in the English schools. We owe thanks to all these people. Certain of the conversations were fairly structured, in that I had a list of topics I wanted people to talk about.

I think we owe the most to Malcolm Griffin (from among the Mossford Green teachers), and Anita Watts and her family, and the Mark Jennings family, from among the Mossford Green parents and former pupils. Of the teachers and school Heads who had taught elsewhere in England: Judith Loughheed, Sheila Andrews, and Gillian Hancock were of especial importance to us.

Finally, some acknowledgment should be given to persons such as Tim Brighouse and Michael Barber, who remember what the English schools were like before the era of the National Curriculum, and who are unwilling to let the matter rest. More power to them. The danger is: that the nation will gradually forget. Our hope is: that there will be some impetus to get that load of bureaucracy off the teachers.

Dr. Bill Rogers is the publisher of this book; Karen Wells was the editor. They provided the best publishing experience of my life. I wish I had found them sooner. I hope that many other authors can get the benefit of their kindness.

INDEX